The Lord Our Habitation

Grace To Build For God

A Story Worth Telling

Now thanks be unto God, which always causeth us to triumph in Christ, and maketh manifest the savour of his knowledge by us in every place

[2 Corinthians 2:14]

SIGNIFICANT SUBJECT VERSES

Jeremiah 31:4 *Again I will build thee, and thou shalt be built*

Acts 17:28 *For in him we live, and move, and have our being;*

John 1 *In the beginning was the Word, and the Word was with God, and the Word was God. ² The same was in the beginning with God. ³ All things were made by him; and without him was not anything made that was made. ⁴ In him was life; and the life was the light of men.*

Hebrews 2:10 *For it became him, for whom are all things, and by whom are all things,*

2 Peter 1:2-3 *Grace and peace be multiplied unto you through the knowledge of God, and of Jesus our Lord,³ According as His divine power hath given unto us all things that pertain unto life and Godliness.*

1 John 1:1 *That which was from the beginning, which we have heard, which we have seen with our eyes, which we have looked upon, and our hands have handled, of the Word of life;…. ²that eternal life,………³ That which we have seen and heard declare we*

Matthew in 11:5 *The blind receive their sight, and the lame walk, the lepers are cleansed, and the deaf hear, the dead are raised up, and the poor have the gospel preached to them.*

Isaiah 12:5 *Sing unto the Lord; for He has done excellent things; this is known in all the earth,*

Revelation 8:1 *I am Alpha and Omega, the beginning and the ending, saith the Lord, which is, and which was, and which is to come, the Almighty.*

Ephesians 2:21-22 *In whom [Christ] all the building fitly framed together groweth unto an holy temple in the Lord: [22] In whom ye also are builded together for an habitation of God through the Spirit.*

Acts 20:32 *And now, brethren, I commend you to God, and to the word of his grace, which is able to build you up, and to give you an inheritance among all them which are sanctified.*

Colossians 2:7 *Rooted and built up in him, and established in the faith, as ye have been taught, abounding therein with thanksgiving.*

Matthew 5:34 *But I say unto you, Swear not at all; neither by heaven; for it is God's throne: [35]Nor by the earth; for it is his footstool:*

Haggai 1:8 *"Go up to the mountains, bring wood and rebuild the temple, that I may be pleased with it and be glorified," says the LORD.*

Deuteronomy 2:7 *For the LORD thy God hath blessed thee in all the works of thy hand: he knoweth thy walking through this great wilderness: these forty years the LORD thy God hath been with thee; thou hast lacked nothing.*

1 Thessalonians 5:11 *Therefore encourage one another and build up one another, just as you also are doing.*

Philippians 1:6 *Being confident of this very thing, that He [God] which hath begun a good work in you [us] will perform it until the day of Jesus Christ:*

Romans 11:36 *For of him, and through him, and to him, are all things: to whom be glory for ever. Amen.*

Colossians 1:16 *For by him were all things created, that are in heaven, and that are in earth, visible and invisible, whether they be thrones, or dominions, or principalities, or powers: all things were created by him, and for him:*

Ascribed Meanings

Grace - good will.

Glory - the visible manifestation of the invisible nature of God.

Lord, I love the habitation of your house and the place where your glory dwells [Psalms 26:8].

First Edition

Copyright © 11 February 2019 Marah Saruchera

All rights reserved. No part of this publication may be reproduced, stored in any retrieval, or transmitted in any form or by any means, electronic, mechanical photocopying, recording or otherwise, without the prior written consent of the author and production team. Reference to or use of the contents is permitted in instances of non-commercial use permitted by copyright law and/or brief quotations.

Where biblical text is referenced, any one of the following bible versions can be used:
King James Version
New King James Version
New International Version
Revised Standard Version
American Standard Version

ISBN 978-1-77906-642-8

Cover Art and Book Design by:
Enhance Graphics
enhancegraphix@gmail.com

CONTENTS

Preface		ii
Introduction		1
Chapter 1	Grateful For Grace	20
Chapter 2	Building For Pharaoh	40
Chapter 3	Building For Self	47
Chapter 4	God Rules	69
Chapter 5	Knowing God, His Holy Spirit and the Lord Jesus	89
Chapter 6	Greater Than The Temple	128
Chapter 7	The Safety Net	148
Chapter 8	The Balm of Gilead	161
Chapter 9	The Magnificent God	184
Chapter 10	The Desert Fountain	198
Chapter 11	Building For God	211
Chapter 12	The Lord Our Habitation	230
Chapter 13	Inexhaustible Grace	239
Chapter 14	Conclusion	243
References		

PREFACE

The grace of God is in everything He does and thinks for and about us.

Grace for us to power shovel for God, in love and with a sound mind.

This book says when man builds, the structure looks good. But man's buildings are built for man by man, for man's glory, with a god connection, yet not for God.

Life, as we know it, has challenges.

These are giant engines of poverty, of disease, of hurt, of betrayal, of anything.

In all and through these challenges, the Lord gives the grace as in Isaiah;

> *28 Have you not known?*
> *Have you not heard?*
> *The everlasting God, the LORD,*
> *The Creator of the ends of the earth,*
> *Neither faints nor is weary.*
> *His understanding is unsearchable.*
> *29 He gives power to the weak,*
> *And to those who have no might He increases strength.*
> *30 Even the youths shall faint and be weary,*
> *And the young men shall utterly fall,*
> *31 But those who wait on the LORD*
> *Shall renew their strength;*
> *They shall mount up with wings like eagles,*

> *They shall run and not be weary,*
> *They shall walk and not faint **[Isaiah 40:28-31]**.*

For those that fear God, everything becomes grace coated.

Under the microscope, our lives become testimonies, we tell our story, the story of grace.

As we walk this earth, we may just be along the path of the cyclone or the tornado, but whatever comes, rooted and built in God, we will survive, because we have been built for strength and purpose.

This book says most people can deal with what they are facing but many cannot deal with what is following them.

The book says we need God to go before us and to cover our rear.

In this book, I say Gideon's three hundred men that lapped river water like dogs were not selected because they were very good.

Gideon's army was not good enough for God to work with, but they were good enough witnesses!

The book says with eyes open, most people fail to see the grace of God; fail to see opportunity to tell their story, because they are too conscious of the crowd.

As much as *we* are building for God, in this grace soaked life, we are simply doing what grace covered people have done before us:-

Noah built the most magnificent ship of all ages – Noah's ark.

Moses oversaw the building of the most magnificent symbol of all time - the Ark of the Covenant.

THEN a man built the TOMB…for himself, yet inadvertently building for God.

Lord, I love the habitation of your house and the place where your glory dwells [Psalms 26:8].

INTRODUCTION

The Lord Our Habitation

David, one of my favourite Bible characters says, *Give thanks unto the LORD, call upon his name, make known his deeds among the people* **[1 Chronicles 16:8]**.

It is because of this verse that David became one of my favourite characters in the Bible.

I have desired to live this life, of thanking God, of calling upon the name of my God, and telling the story of God's grace to me.

David could say what he said because, in my mind, David had a life of hearing God's voice **[1 Samuel 23]**.

The Psalms of David are testimony of his life of praise and worship.

He says *The Lord has done great things for us; whereof we are glad.* [**Psalms 126:3**].

David understood that outside God, there is nothing.

For he [God] spake, and it was done; he commanded, and it stood fast **[Psalms 33:9]**.

The Lord God did the same to me and my life; the Lord spoke a word of life, and everything was established.

Grateful For Grace

Paul, my most inspiring man, says *for in him [God] we live, and move, and have our being [Acts 17:28]*.

To the Romans he said, *for of him, and through him, and to him, are all things: to whom be glory for ever [Romans 11:36]*.

To the Colossians he said, *for by him were all things created, that are in heaven, and that are in earth, visible and invisible, whether they be thrones, or dominions, or principalities, or powers: all things were created by him, and for him [Colossians 1:16]*.

Paul's conviction in the power of God is unchallenged.

It is this power, this awesome power, which I too, rest on.

As Isaiah would say, *for unto us a child is born, unto us a son is given: and the government shall be upon his shoulder: and his name shall be called Wonderful, Counsellor, The mighty God, The everlasting Father, The Prince of Peace. [7] Of the increase of his government and peace there shall be no end [Isaiah 9:6-7]*.

I choose to take habitation in this promise of wonder, of good counsel, of might, of everlastingness, of peace.

Closer to us, I choose to talk about Albert Einstein.

Whilst history is not categorical whether he was Christian or not, he still says "God does not play dice with the universe".

Einstein says further "God tirelessly plays dice under laws which he has himself prescribed" *[Wikipedia.org]*.

Powerful as this statement is, it is an acknowledgement of a "lawgiver", as Einstein would put it, who sets the laws of the universe.

Inadvertently, Einstein is saying, let us give God the praise, the credit, because God created.

As I considered Einstein's statements, I reasoned that Einstein is agreeing with David, and he is agreeing with Paul.

The timing, the placing, the definition, are all God's prerogative.

Then God sent His son. They called Him Jesus and still do.

I too call Him Jesus, my Lord and Saviour.

Jesus came to earth in the manner God wanted and defined.

The Bible says *but when the fullness of the time was come, God sent forth his Son **[Galatians 4:4]***.

So yes, the course of all events is predetermined, by God.

In that predestination, there is a lot of grace!

Grace In Our Choices

Moses says, *I call heaven and earth as witnesses today against you, that I have set before you life and death, blessing and cursing; therefore choose life, that both you and your descendants may live [**Deuteronomy 30:19**].*

What we choose determines our destiny, for good or bad.

The Lord our God works with our choices.

Peter writes;

*Grace and peace be multiplied unto you through the knowledge of God, and of Jesus our Lord,³ According as His divine power hath given unto us all things that pertain unto life and Godliness [**2 Peter 1:2-3**].*

Grace and peace *is* multiplied, as we come to know God and our Lord, Jesus the Christ.

That will be the story of our lives.

Paul says God in us and for us will *do exceeding abundantly above all that we ask or think, according to the power that worketh in us...[Ephesians 3:20].*

Paul is saying God cares that much, such that all our expectations from Him are exceeded by His care and provision.

This is grace.

Grace To Heal

That which was from the beginning, which we have heard, which we have seen with our eyes, which we have looked upon, and our hands have handled, of the Word of life;.... ²that eternal life,..........³ That which we have seen and heard declare we [1 John 1:1].

This was John. John could not hold back. John was addressing the sceptics. He heard, he saw, he touched.

John is saying he was there. Under scrutiny, John's testimony is good.

The blind receive their sight, and the lame walk, the lepers are cleansed, and the deaf hear, the dead are raised up, and the poor have the gospel preached to them [Matthew in 11:5].

John's testimony is corroborated by Mathew.

God will heal our leprosy, the toes, the fingers, and the ears, everything.

God will restore, for He is our Balm of Gilead.

Grace To Plead Our Case

Paul would say, after all his escapades,

And now, brethren, I commend you to God, and to the word of his grace, which is able to build you up, and to give you an inheritance among all them which are sanctified ***[Acts 20:32]***.

God is so in touch with us He says to all,

Come now, let us reason together ***[Isaiah 1:18]***.

This is a good story; God, the Creator of the Universe, the Giver of Life, does reason with man.

The Psalmist says *The earth is the LORD's, and the fullness thereof; the world, and they that dwell therein* ***[Psalm 24:1]***.

Regardless of His power, His might, God gives man opportunity to plead his case, for sanctification, for blessings.

This is why the Bible says,

The steadfast love of the LORD never ceases; his mercies never come to an end; ^{23} they are new every morning; great is your faithfulness ***[Lamentations 3:22-23]***.

It is by God's grace, that we are not destroyed, given all the bad choices we have made.

Therefore *sing unto the Lord; for He has done excellent things; this is known in all the earth.* *[Isaiah12:5]*.

Grace To Build For God

Building for God is not building sand castles, or snow balls.

Building for God is not only building with brick and mortar, or concrete and steel; it is also building your faith in the word of the Lord.

The process of building is the same, brick upon brick, and everything in between.

Building for God is doing all, under the banner of heaven.

It is acknowledging God as God.

It is knowing and understanding the grace the cross of Jesus proffered to us, it is accepting the grace of a magnificent God.

As Jeremiah says of God, *He is the former of all things* ***[Jeremiah 10:16 and Jeremiah 51:19]***.

As I considered Jeremiah's thinking, I came up with this basic understanding of God; before He was, He is.

God's past is His present.

With God's grace, man gets better than expected outcomes, on every front of human existence.

Sustaining Grace

The disciples of Jesus knew the power of God, the power which sustains.

Peter says that God,

[3] According as His divine power hath given unto us all things that pertain unto life and Godliness, through the knowledge of Him that hath called us to glory and virtue ***[2 Peter 1:2-3]***.

It does not matter what it is, physical or mental, social or spiritual, it is God that gave, and it is God that gives.

John, as he was there with Peter, confirms,

*And of his fullness have all we received, and grace for grace [**John 1:16**].*

God's sustaining power is not New Testament power, it is all time power.

Moses says,

*For the LORD thy God hath blessed thee in all the works of thy hand: he knoweth thy walking through this great wilderness: these forty years the LORD thy God hath been with thee; thou hast lacked nothing [**Deuteronomy 2:7**].*

This earth is a wilderness, a great wilderness, with its scorpions, snakes and stones.

It is only grace, which sustains.

Protective Grace

God is our Safety Net.

God says,

*I will go before you, and make all the crooked places straight: I will break in pieces the gates of brass, and cut in sunder the bars of iron [**Isaiah 45: 2**].*

The earth as it is, is enemy territory.

The enemy has planted hedges around us, to obstruct or view, not only of God but everything the Lord has given us.

The enemy has set himself to deny us access to Godliness.

Thank God for grace, to keep fighting.

Paul says.

For the weapons of our warfare are not carnal, but mighty through God to the pulling down of strong holds; ^{5} *Casting down imaginations, and every high thing that exalteth itself against the knowledge of God, and bringing into captivity every thought to the obedience of Christ **[2 Corinthians 10:4]**.*

In the book of Hebrews he says,

*Let us therefore come boldly unto the throne of grace, that we may obtain mercy, and find grace to help in time of need **[Hebrews 4:16]**.*

God's throne is not wood or brass or gold, it is a throne of grace.

This is everyday living, in grace, when we know God and make Him our habitation.

Grace in adversity

Paul says to the Romans,

And we know that all things work together for good to them that love God, to them who are called according to his purpose **[Romans 8:28].**

We may be *troubled on every side, yet not distressed; perplexed, but not in despair;* ⁹ *Persecuted, but not forsaken; cast down, but not destroyed* **[2 Corinthians 4:8-9].**

When our enemies come in like a flood, our God protects.

Grace To Be Built By God

I love this kind of grace, grace to be built by God.

This kind of grace covers every other.

The Lord says to Jeremiah, *Again I will build you, and you shall be built* **[Jeremiah 31:4].**

In God's hands, the pieces come together.

A building site is not a tidy site.

The concrete is being mixed, the earth movers are heaping rubble and fill, the water bowsers are pouring water as and when required.

A building site is a dangerous site.

So is the man that God is building, so are we as we also build each other, for Christ and the glory of our God.

Typical Building Site

*www.canadianarchitect.com/
features/panelization-takes-command
[Accessed 2018]*

The taller the building is going to be, the messier the building process.

For large buildings, even site clearing is a big issue.

Site clearing is not done by hoes; it is done by diesel engine earthmovers and power shovels.

Tall buildings need deep foundations. The soils on which tall buildings stand become important factors.

As tall buildings are exposed to high wind, the type of bracing is critical.

At higher levels the weather is more challenging; the building ought to be stronger than the wind that the building is exposed to.

I like this building analogy a lot. It speaks to me as I also build, for my God.

My assessment of man's everyday life gives me the impression that we are all buildings on very poor soils.

We are construction sites on wrong locations.

We are buildings at different levels of construction.

We need reorientation and reinforcement called grace, so that we are able to stand, tall and magnificent, for our God.

As we all build, the risks and hazards we face from working on construction sites are many, the same apply in building in God, for God.

- Working at height – if working at height, instructions coming from ground level become unreliable. We take instructions from above, because it is only at height, that the height instructions make sense.
- Moving objects – change is critical. The variables in construction need to be factored in at every turn. As God's buildings, we move from one level of faith to another.
- Slips, trips, and falls – some will slip and fall, but most will survive.
- Noise – distractions are many. A construction zone is a war zone.
- Hand arm vibration syndrome - symptoms include numbness, tingling and loss of nerve sensitivity. Without grace, we become disabled.
- Material and manual handling – earthmoving could be energy sapping. We get reinforcements, to keep power-shoveling.
- Collapsing trenches – dug up positions are not always stable. Christianity is not playing marbles. Without grace, our faith, our belief, will collapse.
- Electricity – electricity on site is good, it is necessary, it is not an optional extra, but electricity creates dangerous appliances and positions. Spiritual energy is different with each individual. Different energy levels imply

- different pull power, which on its own can create dangerous connections.
- Airborne fibres and materials – the unexpected can happen.
- Weather – floods, mudslides, storms affect the work, but builds resolve.

Regardless of the challenges, the building ought to continue and the story ought to be told.

A building story is a good story, even in the face of the hazards, as buildings change landscapes.

Regardless of the hazards, no one will be crushed, because there is sufficient grace at the building site:-

- there are safety nets,
- there is a medical team – binding up the wounds, massaging, soothing and calming,
- there are fountains of water - plenty of water, living water.

Above all, we are all buildings on construction sites.

All buildings tell their own story.

Well-built structures tell an enduring story of hope, of survival, of victory.

Lord, I love the habitation of your house and the place where your glory dwells [Psalms 26:8].

CHAPTER 1

GRATEFUL FOR GRACE

Grace In Adversity

Loved by our God, everything we do, everything we are, everything we come across, is grace coated.

The challenge is, sometimes, we fail to see where grace is, how the coating is given, and when the grace will be evident.

We fail to see, to feel, to touch, to hear, and even to smell grace because it is often clad and camouflaged in and by adversity.

We fail to be grateful for grace because life's challenges drive and determine our focus.

We fail to enjoy this grace because we are not in sync with the one who gives grace, the Lord God Almighty, the Creator of the Universe, the Giver of Life – our habitation.

Human beings are God's building.

However, like any building, a condemned building is not fit for use.

- It is grace that God does not condemn us. Instead, God says, *come now, let us reason together [Isaiah 1:18].*

  God loves us, as we are, incapable of loving Him back.

- It is grace that John can say, *and this is the confidence that we have in him, that, if we ask any thing according to his will, he heareth us: ^{15} And if we know that he hears us, whatsoever we ask, we know that we have the petitions that we desired of him [1 John 5:14].*

- It is grace that the cross of Jesus on Calvary gave us life, gave us balance. It gave us privilege to be called sons of God.

- It is grace that we can stand. As Moses stood before Pharaoh, as David stood before Goliath, Paul before Caesar and Joseph of Arimathea before Pilate.

The greatest gift God gave us is said by Paul to Timothy.

Paul says, *for God hath not given us the spirit of fear; but of power, and of love, and of a sound mind [2 Timothy 1:7].*

These three the world now needs and in good measure.

The challenge for man is, what power, what kind of love, what mind.

Power

Power is influence.

There is an adage which says power corrupts and absolute power corrupts absolutely.

When God gave us power, He did not plan to corrupt us, but He gave us power to overcome.

Google.com defined power as the ability or capacity to do something or act in a particular way.

Alternatively, it was defined as the capacity or ability to direct or influence the behaviour of others or the course of events.

This ability to influence or to do come from:

1]. Legitimate Power or positional power.
2]. Expert Power.
3]. Coercive Power.
4]. Referent power.
5]. Reward Power.

Google.com. [2018]
What is power
[Accessed 2018]

All this power, as defined, belongs to God. God has the position, He created and He directs.

God is the source of all power.

God then gave us the ability to do what we do, and the capacity to influence.

It is man's choice, which will determine what he will do with that power.

Everyone has power, big or small, rich or poor, literate or not.

To and for man, power is relative.

Power based on the number of foot soldiers is not enough, for one who has air support will always be better.

When power is from God, it is awesome power. It is power to pray, it is power to forgive, it is power from hope, it is freedom power.

With power from God, we are in a hill position.

A hill position is always better to fight from. It is the greatest power and the only power we will ever need.

That is why Paul says,

⁹ Wherefore God also hath highly exalted him, and given him a name which is above every name:

¹⁰ That at the name of Jesus every knee should bow, of things in heaven, and things in earth, and things under the earth;¹¹ And that every tongue should confess that Jesus Christ is Lord, to the glory of God the Father [Philippians 2:9-11].

Jesus is the name *above* every other name.

Our source of power should never be in doubt, it should never be debatable.

The source is supreme, above every other. Jesus *is* the hill position.

Our power, as Christians, does not come from going to church; although going to church is part of being Christian.

It is power that comes from knowing that built in and on Christ, we are free. Jesus sets free. This is freedom power.

The Bible indicates,

And Jesus came and spake unto them, saying, All power is given unto me in heaven and in earth [Mathew 28:18].

We have the only power broker on our side.

Jesus is alive to all our issues. This is grace.

Hindsight is a perfect science, another saying says.

As and when we look back throughout the journeys of our lives, we can only marvel at what our power broker did, for us and all that belong to us.

When Moses led the children of Israel through the desert, he still stammered, but he got them home, to the borders of Canaan;

When David fled from Saul, he was afraid, yet he could still give Saul his life when he had opportunity to kill him;

When Paul was before the kings in Rome, he was bruised, yet he still endured;

When John was on the island in Patmos, he was hurt, yet he was reassured and could still see and hear his Lord.

These all had opportunity to tell their story – the story of grace.

This is the story told by Moses when he said,

And the L*ORD* *said, Behold, there is a place by me, and thou shalt stand upon a rock* ***[Exodus 33:21]****.*

This is huge.

God wanted Moses to be so close to Him He said there is a place by Him, where Moses could rest.

Grateful For Grace

We have the same privilege; there is a place by our God, where we can find contentment, where we can thrive, where we can live.

A place by the King of Kings, a place by the Lord of Lords, a place by the Creator of the Universe, the Giver of Life, a place by the Almighty!

The Bible says,

And the LORD spake unto Moses face to face, as a man speaketh unto his friend [Exodus 33:11].

That is grace.

The stammering did not matter.

When one talks to one that stammers, they take their time. They leave room for the unexplained. They read between the lines because the other is not eloquent.

God did, for Moses

The Bible also says of Moses,

And Moses said unto the LORD..... ^{16} For wherein shall it be known here that I and thy people have found grace in thy sight? is it not in that thou goest with us? ...... ^{17} And the LORD said unto Moses, I will do this thing also that thou hast spoken: for thou hast found grace in my sight, and I know thee by name [Exodus 33:12-17].

The Lord knows us, not by totem, but by name.

After experiencing the grace of God, Paul said, *¹⁴ and the grace of our Lord overflowed for me* ***[Timothy 1:14]***.

David tells his story too. He fought many wars and triumphed. In the end he says,

And all this assembly shall know that the LORD saveth not with sword and spear ***[1 Samuel 17:47]***.

David tells his story, from Goliath to Absalom, and everything in between.

David will let us know that all his trials were grace coated.

David concludes, *for I will not trust in my bow, neither shall my sword save me* ***[Psalm 44:6]***.

All David needed, was grace in his bow and grace in his sword!

As told by Paul to the Corinthians,

We are troubled on every side, yet not distressed; we are perplexed, but not in despair; ⁹ Persecuted, but not forsaken; cast down, but not destroyed ***[2 Corinthians 4:8-10]***.

Paul knew what grace felt like.

Grateful For Grace

Paul says further,

For I am persuaded that neither death nor life, nor angels nor principalities nor powers, nor things present nor things to come, ^{39} nor height nor depth, nor any other created thing, shall be able to separate us from the love of God which is in Christ Jesus our Lord **[Romans 8:38-39].**

Grace gives strength, of purpose, of mind and body.

Grace makes bold, grace convicts and grace assures.

The Bible says about Pauls journeys,

And the night following the Lord stood by him, and said, Be of good cheer, Paul: for as thou hast testified of me in Jerusalem, so must thou bear witness also at Rome **[Acts 23:11].**

This is huge.

This is powerful and above all, this is grace.

The Lord stood by Paul physically, emotionally, spiritually, in everything.

That kind of story needed Paul to tell. Paul had first-hand experience of the grace of God.

These narratives tell me of the power that governs us, which power propelled man like Moses, David, Paul, John and many more, the earthmovers of our faith.

The same power, the same grace, works in us and for us too.

That is the grace to power shovel for God and in God.

Love

One preacher I have listened to said, "It is an aspect of life that opportunity always puts on an adversary suit" [T.D. Jakes sermon on YouTube].

In this environment, it is hard to love, completely.

My view says love is the most complicated aspect of human existence.

No one on earth truly understands what love is,

No one is capable of completely describing it,

It cannot be imagined, it requires to be experienced,

Love can be difficult to understand,

If love is felt, it can be misleading.

When I looked up the definition of love, I considered this "definition" of love – to love is to act lovingly.

This is what God does. God acts lovingly.

Peter says, *above all, love each other deeply, because love covers over a multitude of sins **[1 Peter 4:8]**.*

The one who truly loves, Jesus of Nazareth, says, *my command is this: Love each other as I have loved you [John15:12]*.

This begs the question – how did Jesus love.

Paul puts it best – he says Jesus is touched with the feeling of our infirmities.

Where we are short, Jesus covers up, when we are sick [and we are sick all the time], Jesus heals; when we err, Jesus forgives, when we die, Jesus resurrects.

The Bible says, *Behold, what manner of love the Father hath bestowed upon us, that we should be called the sons of God [1 John 3]*.

Truly, what manner of love?

Isaiah explained this love when he says,

For unto us a child is born, unto us a son is given: and the government shall be upon his shoulder: and his name shall be called Wonderful, Counsellor, The mighty God, The everlasting Father, The Prince of Peace. ^{7} Of the increase of his government and peace there shall be no end [Isaiah 9:6-9].

It was for us – unto us.

That is love.

Sound mind

The mind or the heart is the most secretive part of a human being. It is defined as

1. the element of a person that enables them to be aware of the world and their experiences, to think, and to feel; the faculty of consciousness and thought..
2. a person's ability to think and reason; the intellect.

Wikipedia.org. [January, 2019]
[Accessed November 7, 2018]

A sound mind is a concerned mind; it is a positive mind-set, focused, all-encompassing, thorough.

It is complete thinking.

Our God says,

For I know the thoughts that I think toward you, saith the LORD, *thoughts of peace, and not of evil, to give you an expected end* ***[Jeremiah 29:11]***.

What we want is a good ending.

God cares about the details of the journey, but it is the end that touches His heart.

A sound mind will give us a good ending, because when we begin right, by God's grace, we will end right.

Science says whatever you desire, you can achieve it using *Mind Power*.

Science says all physical reality is made up of vibrations of energy; even one's thoughts are vibrations of energy.

> *Google.com. Mind Power*
> *[Accessed November 7, 2018]*

Science agrees that one's thoughts have a powerful influence on one's life.

This is not new.

God created the mind and tested Adam in the garden.

And Adam *could* name the animals as God intended them to be named. That is absolute mind power.

The same Adam "knew" Eve as soon as he woke up, yet he had been "sleeping" and had never seen Eve before.

The same mind power has taken man to space and back.

This level of mind power has to be grace coated, because it can precede man's fall from grace.

Paul summarises the issues of the mind by saying,

Let this mind be in you, which was also in Christ Jesus [Philippians 2:5].

The mind will control the power and the love, for without a sound mind, the power and the love are abused.

Amazing Grace

Grace is manifest in God's protection during each moment of time in our lives.

As I was considering God's protective grace, there are four aspects of grace that touched me as a human being, and a child of God.

- **God's assurance and protection**

I have read a little about the American Civil War, and one word that fascinated me was "confederate".

Confederate is a name that seems quite new and exotic, which means allied, associate, joined, united and the like.

I surmise that this was a word coined by God when the Lord said through the prophet Isaiah,

The king of Syria and the king of Israel formed a confederate to fight Judah [Isaiah 7:2].

Thank God for his confederacy with his people.

What these two kings of did not know is that the all-seeing God and the all-knowing God was confederate to Judah.

When the enemy confederate against you, you will need the hill advantage, the God advantage.

That height advantage, the superior air power, only God can give.

The Bible says to reassure,

So shall they fear the name of the Lord from the west, and his glory from the rising of the sun. When the enemy shall come in like a flood, the Spirit of the Lord shall lift up a standard against him. 20 And the Redeemer shall come to Zion, and unto them that turn from transgression in Jacob, saith the Lord [Isaiah59:19-20].

This is an aspect of life that we face every passing day.

The enemy is confederate against the children of God.

The enemy is confederate with the people we love, the people we trust, even the people we pray for.

This is enemy strategy to weaken our resolve to love and serve God.

We need the Lord our God to raise up His standard against the enemy.

God's standard is His law. Breaking the law has consequences, not from man but from God.

The law of God is our protector.

- **God's benevolence and provision**

Solomon says,

*I returned, and saw under the sun, that the race is not to the swift, nor the battle to the strong, neither yet bread to the wise, nor yet riches to men of understanding, nor yet favour to men of skill; but time and chance happeneth to them all **[Ecclesiastes 9:11]**.*

We have been well endowed, with all that pertain to life as we know it, and to Godliness as set by God.

We do not need to be swift in battle, nor strong.

We do not need a lot of wisdom to get bread; we only need to bank on the mind of God towards us.

- **God's design and purpose**

The Psalmist says,

Thine eyes did see my substance, yet being unperfect; and in thy book all my members were written, which in continuance were fashioned, when as yet there was none of them. ¹⁷ How precious also are thy thoughts unto me, O God! how great is the sum of them **[Psalm 139:16-17]**.

Awesome.

All my members were written in the book of God.

The Psalmist goes on to say, we are fearfully and wonderfully made.

The looks do not matter, the colour does not matter, neither the size.

The Lord God saw our substance, so precious were we He needed to make a record.

David asks "Who is man, that God is so mindful of him.

Who really is man?

A man walking is so small; grass in the plains can easily hide him,

Man gets lost so easily in the forest or even in the city he built,

Man can be swept away by knee deep river water,

Man cannot see through things,

Man cannot fly,

Man gets sick so easily,

Man cannot breathe in water, and

Man does not know tomorrow.

Man is just man.

Still, God purposed that man should be just man.

The Bible says,

*Let us hear the conclusion of the whole matter: Fear God, and keep his commandments: for this is the whole duty of man [**Ecclesiastes 12:3**]*

*This people have I formed for myself; they shall shew forth my praise [**Isaiah 43:21**].*

*He hath shewed thee, O man, what is good; and what doth the LORD require of thee, but to do justly, and to love mercy, and to walk humbly with thy God [**Micah 6:8**].*

These verses come quickly to mind; we are God's turnkey projects, God's purpose and design.

It is not about dress codes, but how we dress,

It is not about how we sing, but the songs we sing,

Christianity is not about eloquence in speech, but what and who we speak of.

Christ has already done everything for us.

Outside what Christ gives, there is nothing!

- **God's faithfulness and promise**

God's promises are "Yes" and "Amen".

For all the promises of God in him are *yea, and in him Amen, unto the glory of God by us* ***[2 Corinthians 1:20].***

This is a grace filled statement.

Nahum summarises the faithfulness and promises of God in this statement;

*The LORD is good, a stronghold in the day of distress; He cares for those who trust in Him **[Nahum 1:7].***

Another translation of the Bible puts it this way;

*The Lord is good, a strong hold in the day of trouble; and he knoweth them that trust in him **[Nahum 1:7].***

The book of Numbers adds,

God is not a man, that he should lie; neither the son of man, that he should repent: hath he said, and shall he *not do it? or hath he spoken, and shall he not make it good [**Numbers 23:19-21**].*

So does James,

*¹⁷ Every good gift and every perfect gift is from above, and cometh down from the Father of lights, with whom is no variableness, neither shadow of turning [**James 1:17**].*

Our God is faithful, and He keeps promise.

This is why I say,

Lord, I love the habitation of your house and the place where your glory dwells [Psalms 26:8].

CHAPTER 2

BUILDING FOR PHARAOH

The Great Pyramid

The times I have read the scriptures, especially *Isaiah 43:3*, I have wondered, why does God say He gave Egypt for my ransom?

On searching the internet, I picked that "ransom is a sum of money demanded or paid for the release of a captive".

Google Oxford Online Dictionary

As I considered this definition in the context of Isaiah 43:3, I understood that God paid hugely for the redemption of Israel.

In the same way, God did not spare His precious Jesus, for my comfort.

When the children of Israel came out of Egypt, God literally ran riot on the Egyptians and their Pharaohs.

Israel was chosen, God wanted to ride on their banner.

Egypt, Ethiopia, Sheba. That was the region of influence. It is interesting that God says He gave up these for Israel.

Instead, Israel was going to be the flag bearer.

So what is so particular about Egypt, and why would God give it up, and if He did, how?

History, geography, tourism, and everything else in Egypt is tied to the Pyramids, especially what man has called the great pyramids of Giza.

In addition, the Nile river, though it flows through eleven countries, it is in Egypt that it has a god.

It is recorded that the great pyramid of Giza is the oldest of all the wonders of the world.

The facts about the Great Pyramid of Egypt are revealing:-

- The overall weight of the structure is estimated to be around 5.9 million tons.
- Experts estimate that nearly 2.3 million stone blocks had been used to build this massive structure, with the average weight of each stone block being 7 tons. Some of the stone blocks were as heavy as 30 tons and some weighed well over 50 tons.
- Modern scientists have been baffled by the mortar that was used for the construction of the pyramid. The mortar is way stronger than the rocks that were used and though scientists have actually analyzed the chemical composition of the mortar, they have not been able to reproduce it.
- Inside this great pyramid, the temperature is maintained at a constant and stable 20 degrees Celsius or 68 degrees Fahrenheit. It is fascinating

- that this temperature does never change and is actually equal to earth's average temperature.
- The Great Pyramid sits right on top of the centre of earth's land mass or Earth's geographical centre.
- What are the odds of the Pyramid being accidentally built at earth's geographical centre? Well that's 1 out of 3 billion [1 divided by 3 billion is the probability], because there are actually a billion sites on planet earth that could have housed the Great Pyramid.

Facts and Legend. [December1, 2015]
Great Pyramid of Giza – 60 Interesting Facts To Blow Your Mind.
[Accessed 2018]

As the article on the Great Pyramid indicates, there are absolutely no records found about the Great Pyramid.

No artefacts, no inventory, no drawing or picture – just nothing.

Yet, as internet searches indicate, this is a place visited by more than fourteen million people a year, a place that is estimated to be over 4,500 years old.

In this article on the Great Pyramid of Giza, the researcher writes, "Egyptians, who were known for putting down pictorial history of everything like agriculture to birth to death to prayers to sacrifices to weaving to embalming… they left 3000 years of history for us to decipher".

I figured this is not by accident or chance. I call it Godly interference.

Without any record, there is no replication. Only God has the complete record.

Pharaoh's might had to come to an end, because God decided it was time.

Egypt had had all the privileges of relating in the realms of godliness, but did not know God.

That is why the Bible says,

There they will exclaim, 'Pharaoh king of Egypt is only a loud noise; he has missed his opportunity ***[Jeremiah 46:17].***

The children of Israel knew what the waters of the Nile could do.

Egypt's "fertility" rested on the Nile.

The Bible says,

And the waters shall fail from the sea, and the river shall be wasted and dried up ***[Isaiah 19:5-8].***

The floods of the Nile stopped, and the Nile Delta continues to shrink.

God would not compete with the gods of Egypt. It had to be God and God alone.

For I am the LORD *thy God, the Holy One of Israel, thy Saviour: I gave Egypt for thy ransom, Ethiopia and Seba for thee. ⁴ Since thou wast precious in my sight, thou hast been honourable, and I have loved thee: therefore will I give men for thee, and people for thy life....* ^{7}*Even every one that is called by my name: for I have created him for my glory, I have formed him; yea, I have made him [Isaiah 43].*

Everything that is created, formed and built by God, is for God's glory.

Egypt built the great pyramids, but nothing changed.

The evidence that no Pharaoh was ever buried in the great pyramid says it all – it was all vanity.

^{10} Ye are my witnesses, saith the LORD,.. that ye may know and believe me, and understand that I am he: before me there was no God formed, neither shall there be after me. ^{11} I, even I, am the LORD; and beside me there is no saviour. ^{12} I have declared, and have saved, and I have shewed: therefore ye are my witnesses, saith the LORD, that I am God [Isaiah 43:10-12].

This is huge.

This God, who created, who formed, everything out of nothing, says we are His witnesses.

Yea, before the day was I am he; and there is none that can deliver out of my hand: I will work, and who shall let it? .....^{15} I am the LORD, your Holy One, the creator of Israel, your King. ^{16} Thus saith the LORD, which maketh a way in the sea, and a path in the mighty waters [Isaiah 43:14-16].

The pyramids of Egypt are a reflection of the continuation of the Babel mentality.

The pyramids had a god connection, yet not for God.

This Egyptian project shows man has tremendous capacity to build.

The details of the pyramids are good.

The essence was, man wanted to live in eternity, only he just did not know how.

The Lord God had to give us a way to Him, so that we could know God, as our God. Not as the Egyptians knew Pharaoh.

The Egyptians built good structures; they built for man, for man's glory, with a god connection, yet not for God.

The bible says, when Jesus went back to heaven, he had said in a parable, *occupy till I come [Luke 19:13].*

An expression of occupation is building.

My thinking is building by man is not bad. It is man's expression of self.

The great pyramid of Giza has tunnels inside that go up and down to the king's chamber.

God's relationship with us is not "tunnelled". God comes to our level, to reason with us.

This is our God.

When Noah built the ark, God came down and gave the instructions, when Moses did, the details were specified.

God is different from any other gods.

To whom will you liken Me, or who is My equal?" asks the Holy One [Isaiah 40:25].

From the article Facts and Legends alluded to earlier, on the great pyramid of Giza, the writer states that man ask "was the great pyramid of Giza built by Egyptians or was it the work of some extra-terrestrial life form, far more intelligent than the ancient people?"

That is the question of our time – how does God build and how do man?

When our God builds, there is never any doubt that God did.

Lord, I love the habitation of your house and the place where your glory dwells [Psalms 26:8].

CHAPTER 3
BUILDING FOR SELF

Foundation Uncertain

I know the facts of the great pyramids, and I also know the facts about buildings that tilt.

The buildings that tilt are never designed to tilt, they are built to stand straight.

Buildings that tilt do not tilt in one day, as that would be cause for falling.

Buildings that tilt take time. Years of tilting pass, till, at some stage, they either completely fall, or they sustain their tilted position.

As I searched for a good story of leaning buildings, I came across the Leaning Tower of Pisa. It is an amazing story of resilient builders, and grace.

The leaning tower of Pisa was built on soft ground. The same area is also sandy.

That first submission, for me, was a double no. How could builders, with plans to build a high or tall structure, choose such a site?

Both wet soils and sandy soils do not make buildings stand, without elaborate reinforcement and purpose made engineering designs.

In AD 1173, almost one thousand years ago, these were the places to simply avoid.

The soft and sandy earth could not be good for a multi storey building.

If size is going to be big, then the foundations ought to stand – in time and space.

The Leaning Tower of Pisa has been built over two centuries.

Generations of construction workers, engineers and architects have worked around this building over an incredibly long period.

This tower was first constructed in August 14, 1173.

Measured through the average life span of buildings, this building should have fallen anyway.

Inadvertently, this building has become a tourist attraction.

What I have learnt about the great pyramids is that the millions of tons of stone could not have stood on soft and sandy soils. The size of the pyramid needed a stronger and heavier rock underneath.

Leaning Tower of Pisa

https://en.wikipedia.org/wiki/Leaning_Tower_of_Pisa
Accessed October 12, 2018]

The engineers of Pisa failed in this basic principle – the water table was high, the soils were soft and sandy, so an eight storey building was not going to stand on shallow foundations.

As I considered this Pisa project, my mind created an analogy with God's building projects.

The Lord builds by creating, so that what is built fits into the created structures.

This is the amazing fact about God:-

From the book of Psalms, the Psalmist says,

*¹The earth is the LORD's, and the fulness thereof; the world, and they that dwell therein. ² For he hath founded it upon the seas, and established it upon the floods **[Psalms 24:1-2]***

The earth was created in the beginning of God's creation time; it was created full, with its foundations upon the seas.

The earth was well established upon the floods, the rivers and the lakes.

The 10th century is a long way back. Engineers of that time decided to "mimic" God by building in vlei areas, and the result is what we see, tilted buildings.

The tower of Pisa sat at the wrong place.

Of walking, standing and seating, the Bible says,

*Blessed is the man that walketh not in the counsel of the ungodly, nor standeth in the way of sinners, nor sitteth in the seat of the scornful **[Psalms 1:1]**.*

When one sits at the wrong place, the Lord's blessing one will not get, because the Lord who blesses is simply not there.

*² But his delight is in the law of the LORD; and in his law doth he meditate day and night **[Psalms 1:2]**.*

The law of building does not change. The three elements of construction – cost, time and quality, stand the test of time.

Albert Einstein, alluded to in the introduction of this book, acknowledges there is a lawgiver who determines the variables of life.

The Bible says in the book of Jeremiah, about the house of Israel, Jerusalem and Judah;

Because they have forsaken my law which I set before them, and have not obeyed my voice, neither walked therein [Jeremiah 9:13].

God would make the land desolate and the city ruins.

As God forsook Egypt, Ethiopia and Sheba, because they would not honour God, the same principle, the same law, would apply, even to the people He had chosen so that He, God, would show forth His glory.

From this simple analogy, where you sit is very important.

The Psalmist talks of the ungodly, sinners and the scornful.

I wondered why there is a separation or distinction of persons.

The meanings of these I decided to check out;

See that no one is sexually immoral, or is godless like Esau, who for a single meal sold his inheritance rights as the oldest son [Hebrews 12:16].

This "definition" of ungodly or godless people is quite striking.

When you put Esau into the statement, what we consider as non-consequential becomes the thing that takes away the most important things from our lives.

When one breaks the laws of the lawgiver, and walks in the counsel of the ungodly, then leaning is their end.

Sinners, on the other hand, are those the Bible says in James,

Therefore to him that knoweth to do good, and doeth it not, to him it is sin **[James 4:17]**.

Micah puts goodness into perspective and says.

He hath shewed thee, O man, what is *good; and what doth the LORD require of thee, but to do justly, and to love mercy, and to walk humbly with thy God* **[Micah 6:8]**.

The scornful I thought were inconsequential, but no, they take the energy out of you.

Scornful people are contemptuous, disdainful, disrespectful, mocking.

The Bible says,

The one who plans to do evil will be called a scheming person. A foolish scheme is sin, and the scorner is an abomination to people [Proverbs 24:8].

Scorners are people whose stories are a burden to the ears. They mock and ridicule, people avoid them.

These people that the Psalmist talks about in chapter 1 are like the tower of Pisa.

For more than 800 years the tower of Pisa has been "under construction".

Engineers and contractors still come to the building with "picks and shovels".

The same nature is the tilted mind of those who sit with the scornful. Man and woman alike, we ought to be careful who we walk with, stand with or stand for, and we need to mind how others receive what we say.

It has not helped that many engineers are called to attend to the leaning tower.

Even the 21st century technology has not helped.

As long as the ground is soft, the foundation is weak.

Weak soils will need a lot of reinforcement steel.

God saw us weak and incapable of saving ourselves, incapable of standing straight, and he sent His son Jesus.

The foundations of Pisa

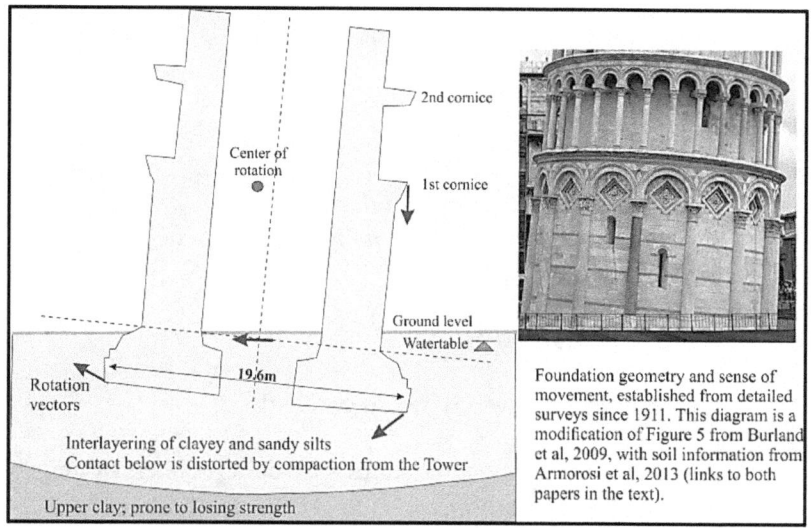

The Foundations of the Leaning Tower of Pisa

https://www.expedia.com/Leaning-Tower-Pisa
[Accessed October 12, 2018]

We got the strength, we got stability, and we got fortitude.

In Jesus, we stand.

As Paul said to Timothy; *[7] for the Spirit God gave us does not make us timid, but gives us power, love and self-discipline **[2 Timothy 1:7].***

The spirit of our God does not make us tilted.

God hath not given us the spirit of fear; but of power, and of love, and of a sound mind **[2 Timothy 1:7]**.

That spirit does not make us fearful; it is a spirit of truth.

God reassures;

As many as received him, to them gave he power to become the sons of God, even to them that believe on his name **[John 1:12]**.

This is the starting point.

Our habitation is where we sit or stand.

Sitting or standing also states our belief system, our values and our aspirations.

People ask where you sit, even when you are standing, or where you stand, even when one is sitting.

A tilted person can fall anywhere; it just depends on which side the water table is higher.

A tilted person cannot be trusted, cannot be relied upon.

Built For Strength

Taipei 101

This building was built to stand the winds and earthquakes of Taipei, in Taiwan.

As an article on the building states, the building was made to withstand lateral forces of nature.

That was an overriding consideration in the architecture and structure of Taipei 101.

As people, our life is very much about standing or falling, when the winds blow, the lateral forces of human nature.

It is part of life for winds to blow. What matters is how we are built.

Only God builds for us to overcome, to triumph, to stand, regardless of how the wind blows.

Winds are devastating. The extent depends on where they hit, when and how.

Winds can come in and with the monsoon; they can come in a tornado or whirlwind.

Winds come, because it is wind season.

Wind can also be just wind, sauntering the leaves of the trees and the grass, or it can be rainstorm driving.

As quoted from K. Haider article, Taiwan is located north of the Philippines and the South China Sea, about

180 km off the south-eastern coast of China, separated from the mainland by the Taiwan Strait.

Taipei is therefore naturally exposed to the wind, and tropical cyclones.

K. Haider. [May 11, 2015] 5 Tallest Buildings in the World.
[Accessed October 12, 2018]

Taipei 101

K. Haider. [May 11, 2015] 5 Tallest Buildings in the World.
[Accessed October 12, 2018]

As weather reporters and investigators say, tropical cyclones use warm, moist air as fuel.

My analogy goes like this:

The Bible requires people who are cold or hot, and not warm. Warmth is middle ground.

Warmth is like being double minded. Warm is being doubtful.

Middle ground underscores indecision.

That warm environment can create dangerous cyclones.

These "tropical cyclones" I equate to poverty, of disease, of hurt, of betrayal, of confusion, of conflict.

These cyclones ride on the warm wind.

In Jesus time, such winds also blew.

The incident of Mark 4 gives a beautiful illustration of what can be, when Jesus is not there, and what is, when God is there.

[37] *And there arose a great storm of wind, and the waves beat into the ship, so that it was now full.* [38] *And he was in the hinder part of the ship, asleep on a pillow: and they awake him, and say unto him, Master, carest thou not that we perish?* [39] *And he arose, and rebuked the wind, and said unto the sea, Peace, be still. And the wind ceased, and there was a great calm.* [41] *And they feared exceedingly, and said one to another, What manner of man is this, that even the wind and the sea obey him* **[Mark 4:36-41]***.*

Like the disciples, we may just be along the path of the cyclone or the tornado.

It is a fact of life that life happens.

Storms can come, not of our own making.

As various stories have been told, the most basic rule in a cyclone or tornado situation is – stay inside.

This is so simple, yet so many people die because of tropical storms.

In cyclone country, preparation saves lives.

We need to make sure Jesus is in the same boat with us. Whether He sleeps or not, it should never be our concern.

Jesus ought to be within earshot, so that when we call, He hears.

The worst that can happen is – we swim to safety.

The winds of life can rise so easily when one stays in neutral position, in the warm areas. There is simply no traction.

Gears in neutral position do not work. In neutral position, there is no controlled acceleration and there is no controlled stopping.

Neutral positions are dangerous, in case of emergency, the brakes are unresponsive.

As the weather reporters say, beware of the calm "eye".

That is the centre of the storm. The one area that appears so ok, beware!

Taipei 101 is a lonely tall building in the middle of low level buildings. It is too exposed.

Although naturally designed to be that tall, that visible, it is too tall for its location.

We need a life engineer with extra wisdom, who can read the strength of the wind, and also knows our strengths and weaknesses.

We need an engineer who knows where and how we need reinforcement steel.

We have that engineer with extra acumen, in our Lord and saviour, Jesus the Christ.

This, I conclude, is because most people, for their surroundings, are too tall and exposed, just like Taipei 101.

Some are tall and exposed, not by their own will, but by God's design.

In warm climates, they become the target of life's storms, they need a hiding place.

In God, we have a hiding place. The Lord our God says,

Come, my people, enter thou into thy chambers, and shut thy doors about thee: hide thyself as it were for a little moment, until the indignation be overpast [Isaiah 26:20].

Burj Khalifa

An article on Burj Khalifa indicates; this building has 162 floors, 30,000 residences, along with 9 hotels and a huge shopping mall. It was built to accommodate.

There are a total 57 elevators and 8 escalators, and the elevators are big enough to take in 12-14 people.

The building stands at 2,717 feet of height.

Modern Dubai +Burj Khalifa Guide Tour
[Accessed October 2018]

This building was built for the desert.

Deserts are always a challenge.

Deserts are dry. In particular, their soils are dry.

Deserts are barren. Very little grows in the desert.

By God's design, deserts also have oases.

As generally understood, desert climate is one in which there is a net deficit of water or moisture.

Life, can be a desert, dry and barren.

The desert dunes, so attractive from a distance, are so wanting; they leave people parched and thirsty.

What grows in the desert is that which God created *for* the desert.

Burj Khalifa is a building that was constructed to give reputation to the desert city of Dubai.

True to the intentions of the visionaries, Burj Khalifa has given to Dubai a reputation for self-sufficiency and financial muscle. Burj Khalifa stands for Arabian excellence.

It is designed to avoid wind pressure, and with a wall cladding to reflect the heat of the desert.

These designers and engineers of Burj Khalifa made special mention of what they called "three some power in building".

Modern Dubai +Burj Khalifa Guide Tour
[Accessed October 2018]

From this article, my analogy is;

Life well lived is life lived within the three-some power of the Lord almighty.

That three-some power breaks all winds, even desert winds.

Burj Khalifa

Destination Dubai. [2016]Modern Dubai +Burj Khalifa Guide Tour. *[Accessed October 2018]*

Not all deserts are the same. There are perennial deserts and there are seasonal deserts.

Perennial or seasonal, all are deserts.

The effects of the deserts and their bearing on our lives leave the same debilitating effects, regardless of location.

God changes deserts, He makes rivers flow.

God changes desert seasons.

God makes the rainy clouds.

God opens up the earth so springs of water can start flowing.

He is God.

The geophysics of building man is well known by God. Building is not man's domain, but belongs to God.

God built everything that stands, that endures. He builds on Himself.

As Isaiah would say,

Hast thou not known? hast thou not heard, that *the everlasting God, the LORD, the Creator of the ends of the earth, fainteth not, neither is weary? there* is *no searching of his understanding **[Isaiah 40:28]**.*

As I kept reading to understand the laws governing building, I accepted that most building is purposeful; building is an answer to challenges, to questions.

Buildings are solutions to problems.

As much as building has always been fascinating, I was surprised by,

Project 2018 - Parker Solar Probe

This is a space ship built to understand how the sun "hots up", built to find answers.

It was evident that some of the best physicists of this century have been working on getting "to know the sun".

In their world, they want to answer what they called the "remaining questions" on how the sun shines beyond the earth!

The team describes the sun as a dynamic and magnetically active star, which sends magnetized material outward, enveloping our solar system far beyond the orbit of Pluto and influencing every world along the way.

NASA Prepares to Launch Parker Solar Probe, a Mission to Touch the Sun. [Accessed November 9, 2018]

This team acknowledges they cannot understand the influence of the sun without understanding the sun itself.

In summary, they had three questions on what they called "our star"

1. The mystery of the acceleration of the solar wind, the Sun's constant outflow of material.

They want to know the point – as-yet unobserved – where the solar wind is accelerated to supersonic speeds.

2. Scientists hope to learn the secret of the corona's enormously high temperatures.

The indications are that the visible surface of the Sun is about 10,000 F – but, for reasons they do not fully understand, the corona is hundreds of times hotter, spiking up to several million degrees F.

As reported, "It's a bit like if you walked away from a campfire and suddenly got much hotter,"

3. They want to reveal the mechanisms at work behind the acceleration of solar energetic particles, which can reach speeds more than half as fast as the speed of light as they rocket away from the Sun.

My analogy is this:

This space project illustrates what man has always wanted to know – mysteries and secrets about God.

Man wants a revelation of the mechanisms behind God's creation, so that they can also build for themselves.

My assertion is this; it does not matter how intelligent man becomes, there are issues and truths which will remain in the realm of God.

God has given us all that we need.

He has given us everything pertaining to life and Godliness, but we will never understand the mechanisms behind – the mysteries and the secrets belong to God.

God is God.

God is the Creator of the Universe, He is the Giver of Life, He is the Former of all things.

The report goes further to say "a NASA astronaut, Scott Kelly, has released a photo book titled "Infinite Wonder", after spending 340 days on an International Space Station".

As I read this report, I kept thinking, Scott Kelly is right, infinite wonder is how God builds – from the inside out.

Amazing Grace

As I was at pains to understand how man builds, for himself, outside God, I thought of the many engineers that have worked on and the tourists that have visited the Leaning Tower of Pisa.

I kept asking why the leaning tower of Pisa has not fallen over.

God cares, even for the tilted.

As K. Haider [May 11, 2015] would ask, can Taipei 101 continue to stand, can it withstand the winds that it cannot control?

I reasoned, yes, for as long as the Lord God says it shall.

Then, of Burj Khalifa, I remarked - man is so good – at imitating God.

Yes, I say, man is ingenious when man looks up to God for inspiration.

Man is ingenious when man looks up to the three some power of heaven.

Man should worship God, because God is too wonderful for us.

Lord, I love the habitation of your house and the place where your glory dwells [Psalms 26:8].

CHAPTER 4

GOD RULES

The Three-Some Power Of Heaven

The whole Bible, from Genesis to Revelation, is a narration, a declaration and a summation of who God is.

I will pick a few texts;

The Lord God says to John in the book of Revelation,

I am Alpha and Omega, the beginning and the ending, saith the Lord, which is, and which was, and which is to come, the Almighty. He lives from everlasting to everlasting ***[Revelation 1:8]***.

This Lord God is in all the time of the ages past.

The Psalmist says,

The LORD hath prepared his throne in the heavens; and his kingdom ruleth over all ***[Psalms 103:19]***.

Jesus says *I and* my *Father are one **[John 10:30]***.

This therefore means, as much as we talk about God, we cannot separate Jesus from His father.

John, a disciple of Jesus, says,

*¹ In the beginning was the Word, and the Word was with God, and the Word was God.² The same was in the beginning with God.³ All things were made by him; and without him was not any thing made that was made.⁴ In him was life; and the life was the light of men [**John 1:1-4**].*

Of Jesus, Phillip said to Nathaniel ....*Come and see **[John 1: 46]**.*

When Phillip saw Jesus, he knew this man was different.

Jesus spoke intentionally, all the time,

Jesus walked with purpose.

Jesus was built differently; Jesus was born of the Father.

As John would later report,

*That which was from the beginning, which we have heard, which we have seen with our eyes, which we have looked upon, and our hands have handled, of the Word of life;.... ²that eternal life,.........³ That which we have seen and heard declare we **[1 John 1:1]**.*

Mathew concurred,

*The blind receive their sight, and the lame walk, the lepers are cleansed, and the deaf hear, the dead are raised up, and the poor have the gospel preached to them **[Matthew in 11:5]**.*

This man Jesus would rule not just in Judea, Samaria, Galilee and all the cities he went to and passed through, he rules through to eternity.

Jesus has dominion. Jesus has the power.

Jesus is the Word of God, Jesus is the Law.

What you see about and in Jesus compels, persuades.

John is explaining the supremacy of God. God is the beginning and the end.

His jurisdiction is beyond our capacity to think or imagine; He is self-governing; He is self-existing.

This, John says, we have heard.

John heard how God parted the waters of the red sea, how he brought the sweet water blessing at Marah, how manna fell from heaven, how the east wind brought the quails to the desert.

John had heard how the road to Canaan was lit by fire from heaven during the night, he had heard how the clouds covered and protected God's own from the sun.

John had heard, and then John saw. John saw truth that delivers and grace that covers.

John says he looked upon these and touched them.

God was building His case. For me and for you, that we may also believe, that He is God.

Paul saw the same and calls it salvation. In a way, Paul read from the same book that John read.

Paul then says,

Neither is there salvation in any other: for there is none other name under heaven given among men, whereby we must be saved [Acts 4:12].

This man, whom everyone could not resist when He spoke, is the master builder. He makes.

He makes dead situations alive again.

Project Babel

The story of the tower of Babel is quite old. It is history.

As is often said, we learn from the past. History informs the present.

What man does, on a daily basis, is derived from fear.

Fear of the known and the unknown, the visible and invisible, the present and the future.

Man wants to "cover" himself, yet he is so much in plain view of God.

Man can only operate through hindsight, that is, when and if he remembers!

Man is fearful of God, not the fear that comes with or from respecting God.

Man flees from God, because man fears the consequences of disrespecting God, yet man wants and need God.

In a way, this indicates man does not understand God.

The Lord God wants to relate to man, to speak with him and to him, to bless him with everything that pertains to life and Godliness.

God avails Himself, to man, in every moment of time, but man is sceptical.

Man is unbelieving, doubtful, unconvinced.

That is why man decided a tower would be good.

This brick and mortar tower was what the flood survivors thought would cover them from God.

Thousands of years later, man is still of the same mind, let us build, perhaps not on planet earth but on Mars!

The Bible says,

*And they said, Go to, let us build us a city and a tower, whose top may reach unto heaven; and let us make us a name, lest we be scattered abroad upon the face of the whole earth **[Genesis 11:4]**.*

*They said to one another, "Come, let us make bricks and burn them thoroughly." And they used brick for stone, and they used tar for mortar **[Genesis 11:3]**.*

In these passages, man is afraid of being scattered and alternatively, of being flooded.

In the process, these men want to make a name for themselves.

The reasons are lame, because these people knew God was God Almighty, all powerful, yet they believe they can truly "beat" God.

This thinking is with man even in this day and age.

Man is building, sometimes even in the name of God, yet not for God.

Man builds for himself.

Men's errands to Mars and the rest of the planet are meant to save man from the "wrath to come".

Whether that wrath comes through climate change or apocalypse as understood by man's imagination, does not matter.

Man wants to live as long as possible, yet not on the terms of the Almighty God.

God, by His infinite grace, still looks on as man builds.

Men after the flood had a very good idea of who God was. They knew where on the ladder of existence God took residence. High up in the heavens.

They feared what this God could and would do, the next time He was not happy.

These men understood God in the context of sin, as the Bible says,

*For our God is a consuming fire **[Hebrews 12:29]**.*

Man after the flood wanted to escape another flood, and man now wants to escape the fire.

Project Babel was started by Noah's grandchildren.

They were right in their finite understanding of God, yet so very wrong about God.

I asked myself as to who was supposed to be impressed by their tower - God?

This is the nature of man. Man does not see the grace that saved him from the flood, or even the magnificence of the ark that floated, but man sees grace as an opportunity to challenge God.

Biblical studies record that the Tower of Babel "was begun about 700 years after the flood, and there were about 2,354 years from the beginning of the world to the confusion of the Tower of Babel.

Computations indicate the tower was built over a period of 107 years.*

> *Wikipedia.org.https://en.wikipedia.org/wiki/Tower_of_Babel*
> *[Accessed November 9, 2018]*

The same thinking that fed the Babel vision is with man today.

Monumental structures pick up our pride, irrespective of religion, age, race or education.

It is the same mentality that led to the building of Taipei 101 and Burj Khalifa – a name.

The same structures also pacifies us regarding the things of God,

We create for ourselves a sense of permanency.

At times the physical structures give to man a sense of achievement, subtle.

We assess ourselves against what God has created,

The Bible says in Jeremiah;

Thus saith the LORD, which giveth the sun for a light by day, and *the ordinances of the moon and of the stars for a light by night, which divideth the sea when the waves thereof roar; The LORD of hosts is his name [Jeremiah 30:35].*

As in the Parker Solar Project, man wants to understand the ordinances, the decrees, the laws that govern the sun, God's creation, an endeavour which is outside the realm of man.

In that project, the basic thinking is correct, man can only understand how the sun works by understanding the sun itself.

The same applies to God. To understand how God works, creates and builds, we ought to understand God Himself.

In the Babel experiment, as I prefer to call this escapade by Noah's grandchildren, the Bible does not say how high the tower was when the Lord intervened.

God intervened so man would not destroy himself, as *nothing would be restrained from them, which they have imagined to do [Genesis 11: 6].*

This was grace.

The flood had come because man's imagination had become so bad, man was thinking wrong all the time.

Even at Babel, the thinking was still wrong.

Men wanted to build up to "high heaven"!

Everything about that tower in that city spelt impending disaster.

What these men were trying to prevent is what then directly resulted from their actions; confusion followed and people were scattered upon the face of all the earth.

It is grace when man builds in God and for God.

God builds, not with brick and mortar, steel or concrete.

God builds with His word, with His Holy Spirit.

Restoration

After the Babel project, the confused people, generation after generation, kept wondering, in thought and practice, until God sent them into exile.

Yet God still had love for them, compassion, God still cared.

He says in Jeremiah, even in exile, my people can still

⁵ Build ye houses, and dwell in them; and plant gardens, and eat the fruit of them; ⁷ And seek the peace of the city whither I have caused you to be carried away captives, and pray unto the LORD for it: for in the peace thereof shall ye have peace. ...¹¹ For I know the thoughts that I think toward you, saith the LORD, thoughts of peace, and not of evil, to give you an expected end.¹² Then shall ye call upon me, and ye shall go and pray unto me, and I will hearken unto you.¹³ And ye shall seek me, and find me, when ye shall search for me with all your heart.¹⁴ And I will be found of you, saith the LORD [Jeremiah 29:5-14].

This is an awesome passage of scripture.

It is God saying, salvation comes from the Father.

God says I will bring you back, in the process of time.

God says whilst there, pray, and I will hear, and give you peace.

God says He can be trusted.

God says He cares.

God says He will build back,

Again I will build thee, and thou shalt be built [Jeremiah 31:4], says the Lord.

That is why Paul says to the Corinthians *for we are God's fellow workers; you are God's field, God's building [1 Corinthians 3:9].*

God has a termination date for man.

A date that separates those He built and the confusion of Babel.

God's Foundations Are Sure

Building is a process that begins with the foundations.

When the foundations are not right, the buildings fall or are tilted.

At the tower of Pisa, for more than 800 years engineers are trying to sort out the foundations.

The foundations that God builds are sure. God's word is the surest foundation ever laid.

The Psalmist says *for he spake, and it was done; he commanded, and it stood fast* ***[Psalm 33:9].***

God is not overly impressed with physical buildings.

Paul knew the same and said if it is about cities and towers, the one God builds is not built by hands; the word of God does the building.

The Lord God, our builder, knows where the special foundations are laid, not through soil testing, but He knows because he creates all fit for purpose, for circumstance, for time.

God knows how the physical relate, the heavens and the earth.

God also knows how these relate in the spiritual.

God knows how relationships are connected,

God knows what material, how strong, how high, and how deep.

This is our God, who builds for eternity.

The Lord God knows what type of concrete and its maturing period,

How much water and how often,

God does not make a mistake.

God's mixing ratios are exact,

His dimensions are specific,

The shapes are accurate – if it is a square, it is a perfect square.

This is our God.

The Lord, Our Dwelling Place

With our God, all building structures are purpose made, and the owner states for what use.

Whilst the Lord God is building us, he has given us opportunity to also build each other.

Built by God, we can only build in God, for the Lord God, is our dwelling place.

*The eternal God is thy dwelling-place, And underneath are the everlasting arms **[Deuteronomy 33:27]**.*

The Psalmist confirms the privilege of being built by God.

*7 A thousand shall fall at thy side, and ten thousand at thy right hand; but it shall not come nigh thee. 8 Only with thine eyes shalt thou behold and see the reward of the wicked. 9 Because thou hast made the LORD, which is my refuge, even the most High, thy habitation **[Psalms 91:7-9]**.*

Other building projects are turnkey projects.

The owner does not do much, the contractor does.

When complete, the owner and user are given the keys and the transaction is complete.

We are God's turnkey projects, Jesus is the contractor. Jesus will work on us until we are ready for heaven.

Building projects are as diverse as building uses.

Some are long term, centuries and generations in the making; some are almost day projects, like building a cabin.

Jesus alludes to building in Mathew. All building has costs.

What price is the Owner willing to pay?

There is collateral in building. What is forgone.

Jesus was the collateral in our redemption, in our building.

For a moment, God "separated" from His son, so that we are perfected in our knowledge of the way, the truth and the life that our God, the everlasting God, desires of us and in us.

Remembering that Jesus said Him and His Father were one, the Lord God bended and still bends over backwards for us to be built, because He cares, He loves.

This concept remains; the Lord God is out habitation, our dwelling place.

In Jesus, the one greater than the temple that Solomon built, we have a hiding place.

Jesus is our Lord Protector.

John the revelator says,

And I heard a great voice out of heaven saying, Behold, the tabernacle of God is with men, and he will dwell with them, and they shall be his people, and God himself shall be with them, and be their God ***[Revelation 21:3-4].***

We tabernacle in our God, not in the physical structure that man built, not even in the one Solomon built, but the one God built.

God wants to be right there besides us, like He said to Moses, there is a place by Him.

Our joy, our pride, should be sitting right there by the Lord – because there is nowhere better!

God says to Moses,

Then have them make a sanctuary for me, and I will dwell among them. ⁹ Make this tabernacle and all its furnishings exactly like the pattern I will show you ***[Exodus 25:8-9].***

God's building and buildings are of a particular type, a particular design. They are built for eternal purpose.

Moses would say during the exodus from Egypt to Canaan,

Thou shalt bring them in, and plant them in the mountain of thine inheritance, in the place, O LORD, which thou hast made for thee to dwell in, in the Sanctuary, O LORD, which thy hands have established **[Exodus 15:17].**

God desires, that we are purposeful beings, built and planted by the Lord.

Isaiah then says,

1 The Spirit of the Lord GOD is upon me; because the LORD hath anointed me to preach good tidings unto the meek; he hath sent me to bind up the brokenhearted, to proclaim liberty to the captives, and the opening of the prison to them that are bound;2 To proclaim the acceptable year of the LORD, and the day of vengeance of our God; to comfort all that mourn;3 To appoint unto them that mourn in Zion, to give unto them beauty for ashes, the oil of joy for mourning, the garment of praise for the spirit of heaviness; that they might be called trees of righteousness, the planting of the LORD, that he might be glorified **[Isaiah 61:3].**

The Lord has built a dwelling place for us to run to in all the storms and challenges of this life.

In mourning we run to God and are comforted.

In chains we run to God and are set free.

Sad, we run to God and our spirits are lifted.

Hurting, we run to God and are healed.

Exposed, we run to God and we are covered.

The Lord God is our habitation, our hiding place.

I want to believe and proclaim that it is not in vain that we worship God.

As the Psalmist says,

*Those that be planted in the house of the LORD shall flourish in the courts of our God **[Psalms 92:13]**.*

When we are overwhelmed, as the Psalmist says,

*From the end of the earth will I cry unto thee, when my heart is overwhelmed: lead me to the rock that is higher than I. 3 For thou hast been a shelter for me, and a strong tower from the enemy. 4 I will abide in thy tabernacle for ever: I will trust in the covert of thy wings **[Psalms 61:2-4]**.*

Our strong tower, our shelter, is God almighty.

Godly Standards

God will dwell where his standards are met.

The world has building standards, for strength and for beauty, how much more the Creator of the Universe?

What God has established is pure, it is awesome.

As I was marvelling at God's creation, the Mandarin Duck just struck a chord.

This is how God builds – flawless.

Mandarin Duck

https://www.puzzlewarehouse.com/Exotics-Mandarin-Duck-50935aan-2.html [Accessed December 12, 2018]

When we are built in God and for God, we will be glorious.

Our conduct unaltered by fame or fortune, our thinking uninterrupted by poverty or pain.

When the Lord was done with His creation, He said it was good.

Rogue characters like Saul were built and their names changed.

God likes physical buildings, but He loves man.

For the physical, He said and it was established, He commanded and it stood fast.

For man, God takes His time.

When God is done with man, everything is out and open to glorify God.

When God is finished with building man, no one gets tilted.

The Solar project is just telling us – man refuses or chooses not to acknowledge and worship God, yet man is inadvertently, looking for God.

Lord, I love the habitation of your house and the place where your glory dwells [Psalms 26:8].

CHAPTER 5

KNOWING GOD, HIS HOLY SPIRIT AND THE LORD JESUS

Almighty God

God and Godliness is not a concept.

Godliness is the difference between life and death.

Paul said to the Athenians;

*^{23} as I passed by, and beheld your devotions, I found an altar with this inscription, TO THE UNKNOWN GOD. Whom therefore ye ignorantly worship, Him declare I unto you. ^{24} God that made the world and all things therein, seeing that he is Lord of heaven and earth, dwelleth not in temples made with hands; ^{25} Neither is worshipped with men's hands, as though he needed any thing, seeing he giveth to all life, and breath, and all things;...^{28} For in him we live, and move, and have our being; as certain also of your own poets have said, For we are also his offspring **[Acts 17:22-28]**.*

What a summary, of God.

Paul is paraphrasing what he knows of God.

It is a bold statement from someone who once was, and now is.

Paul is saying his God created, He is the Giver of Life. No one moves if He has not said so. There is no life or being outside God.

Who God is, can be very personal. To one He is;

- El-Ohim - Genesis 1:1 – God was the True God
- El-Elyon- Genesis 14:19 God is The Most High
- El-Roi - Genesis 16:13 He is The Lord Who Sees
- El-Shadai - Genesis 17:1 The Almighty God
- Jireh - Genesis 22:14 The Provider
- Rapha - Exodus 15:26 The Healer
- Nissi - Exodus 17:15 My Banner
- Shalom - Judges 6:24 My Peace
- Raah - Psalms 23:1 My Shepherd
- Tsidken - Jeremiah 23:6 My Righteousness
- Shamah - Ezekiel 38:45 Who Is There
- Alpha and Omega - Revelation 1:8 The Beginning and the End

This omnipotent God, this all-seeing God, is so caring, so loving and so full of grace.

None can adequately describe God, for He is self-existing.

God is infinite.

[14] God said to Moses, "I AM WHO I AM. This is what you are to say to the Israelites: 'I AM has sent me to you **[Exodus 3:14]**.

I am Who I am, Lord of all.

David says of God;

O Lord, thou hast searched me, and known me. [2] Thou knowest my down sitting and mine uprising, thou understandest my thought afar off. [3] Thou compassest my path and my lying down, and art acquainted with all my ways. [4] For there is not a word in my tongue, but, lo, O LORD, thou knowest it altogether.. [6] Such knowledge is too wonderful for me; it is high, I cannot attain unto it. [7] Whither shall I go from thy spirit? or whither shall I flee from thy presence? [8] If I ascend up into heaven, thou art there: if I make my bed in hell, behold, thou art there. [9] If I take the wings of the morning, and dwell in the uttermost parts of the sea; [10] Even there shall thy hand lead me, and thy right hand shall hold me. [11] If I say, Surely the darkness shall cover me; even the night shall be light about me. [12] Yea, the darkness hideth not from thee; but the night shineth as the day: the darkness and the light are both alike to thee **[Psalms 139:1-12]**.

David and Paul's understanding of God gives us the courage to go on, regardless of all the challenges and issues of life.

David and Paul lived in very different ages of time, yet their understanding of God is equally awesome.

David says *⁶ such knowledge is too wonderful for me; it is high, I cannot attain unto it **[Psalms 139:6]**.*

David is looking at his life and says God has surpassed all his expectations; there is no hiding from God, yet God is our hiding place.

Paul, who lived hundreds of years after David, says,

*²⁸ For in him we live, and move, and have our being **[Acts 17:28]**.*

Paul is at a loss of words to describe our God and how we can relate to Him. Paul is saying; we are complete in God.

There is peace in the knowledge of God as the Almighty God.

With that kind of knowledge of God, trusting Him, believing Him, like Paul, we can stand before the Caesars of this world.

Equally, like David, we can come clean with our God, as the Lord speaks to our faith as in Isaiah, when He says our righteousness is of Him ***[Isaiah 54:17]**.*

We can never be right on our own, we can never do good outside God's enabling.

When we are supposed to pray, He whispers into our hearts and minds to pray, and He creates the opportunity, the environment and even the place where we ought to pray.

He is an awesome God. He gave us all so that we can live in victory.

He is our hiding place. All day and all times, our God rides on our banner.

Merciful God

This God described by Paul is the Lord, who said to Moses,

*And let them make me a sanctuary; that I may dwell among them [**Exodus 25: 8**].*

To think that man could build anything that God could and would inhabit is beyond imagination. It is too wonderful for us, we cannot attain it!

Paul says this God does not dwell in anything made by the hand of man, but God asks Moses and the congregation to build Him a dwelling place, a sanctuary, as if God needed to be preserved.

As I considered the substance of God's instructions to Moses, I figured, yes, God needed to be preserved; He needed His presence to be unspoilt.

The Bible says the Lord's presence fills the whole earth; heaven is His throne, and the earth is His footstool.

How then could God dwell in a *two cubits and a half shall be the length thereof, and a cubit and a half the breadth thereof, and a cubit and a half the height thereof [Exodus 25:10].*

God, in His power and in His glory, could and would not dwell in temples and sanctuaries made by hand of man.

God was asking Moses to keep His laws of Exodus 20, unspoilt, preserved.

This is powerful. Our God, is the Lord, He is Jehovah.

God's presence is in His law. God's law is righteous; it fills the heavens and the earth.

David was right, no one can hide from God's Law, it is eternal, it is everywhere, even in the depths of hell, as David would say of God's presence, it is there.

In the light of day, in the deep darkness, God's law is there.

The darkness cannot hide our God. God's Law is in His Word; the word of truth.

The Psalmist says, *thy word* is *a lamp unto my feet, and a light unto my path* ***[Psalms 119:105]***.

Thy word is true from the beginning: and every one of thy righteous judgments endureth for ever ***[Psalms 119:160]***.

This is the Word of Hebrews chapter 4.

^{12} For the word of God is quick, and powerful, and sharper than any two-edged sword, piercing even to the dividing asunder of soul and spirit, and of the joints and marrow, and is a discerner of the thoughts and intents of the heart. ^{13} Neither is there any creature that is not manifest in his sight: but all things are naked and opened unto the eyes of him with whom we have to do. ^{14} Seeing then that we have a great high priest, that is passed into the heavens, Jesus the Son of God, let us hold fast our profession. ^{15} For we have not an high priest which cannot be touched with the feeling of our infirmities; but was in all points tempted like as we are, yet without sin. ^{16} Let us therefore come boldly unto the throne of grace, that we may obtain mercy, and find grace to help in time of need ***[Hebrews 4:10-16]***.

So man would build a sanctuary, for the Word, that is the Son of God, who is with God and in God.

Amazing grace!

God, faithful and true, asks:

Thus saith the LORD, The heaven is my throne, and the earth is my footstool: where is the house that ye build unto me? and where is the place of my rest? ***[Isaiah 66:1]***.

This was after the children of Israel, the people God had chosen for the manifestation of God's power and glory, had chosen to worship other gods.

God then asked, through Isaiah, what happened to my law?

Paul, as he understood God, was inspired to quote the same scripture of Isaiah.

Heaven is my throne, and earth is my footstool: what house will ye build me? saith the Lord: or what is the place of my rest? ***[Acts 7:49]***.

The Gentile people Paul was preaching to had to know this God too.

The Gentiles were living the same life the chosen generation of the children of Israel had lived during the time of Isaiah the prophet, they were idol worshippers.

These also needed God's Law introduced and preserved among them.

Mathew quotes Jesus saying,

But I say unto you, Swear not at all; neither by heaven; for it is God's throne: ^{35}Nor by the earth; for it is his *footstool: neither by Jerusalem; for it is the city of the great King [Matthew 5:34].*

Jesus was and is the son of the father, yet they are one.

Jesus is sending a message; we cannot take God's name in vain. God is omnipresent.

Jesus was simply going back to God's Law. The law He knew so well. The law He lived by.

When the Lord Jesus says abide in Me and I in you, God is saying, let the law live in you as it is in Me and is Me.

Jesus says,

Whoever abides in me and I in him, he it is that bears much fruit, for apart from me you can do nothing. 6 If anyone does not abide in me he is thrown away like a branch and withers; and the branches are gathered, thrown into the fire, and burned. 7 If you abide in me, and my words abide in you, ask whatever you wish, and it will be done for you. 8 By this my Father is glorified, that you bear much fruit and so prove to be my disciples. 9 As the Father has loved me, so have I loved you [John 15:4-9].

God's Law is God's presence with us and in us.

God knows the specifications for us to abide in Him.

God really wanted the ark in the tabernacle to be that specific size and shape and of that material.

Just so Moses was not in doubt, he was shown the original.

As the Bible says,

*According to all that I shew thee, after the pattern of the tabernacle, and the pattern of all the instruments thereof, even so shall ye make it **[Exodus 25:9]**.*

*And thou shalt put into the ark the testimony which I shall give thee **[Exodus 25:16]**.*

This means the sanctuary that God was talking about was not entirely physical. It was built for purpose. It was a message; it was a letter of intent.

God wanted to remind us of His presence, always. The law would be the testimony of God's grace.

The word of God says the tabernacle of God is with man. It is the evidence that God's tabernacle, God's dwelling place, God's Law, is with man.

As John says in Revelation,

And I heard a great voice out of heaven saying, Behold, the tabernacle of God is with men, and he will dwell with them, and they shall be his people, and God himself shall be with them, and be their God. ***[Revelation 21:3]**.*

This is the story of our lives.

The Bible says God wants to commune with us, not anyhow, not any or everywhere, but above the mercy seat.

The Lord God says to Moses,

*And there I will meet with thee, and I will commune with thee from above the mercy seat **[Exodus 25:22]**.*

This is profound.

I think of this Bible verse and relate it to David's message of Psalms 103.

David could only write what he saw and what he heard, in his time.

Psalms 103 is how David experienced this communion above the mercy seat. He says;

- *God forgiveth all thine iniquities; God healeth all thy diseases;*
- *God redeemeth thy life from destruction; God crowneth thee with loving-kindness and tender mercies;*
- *God satisfieth thy mouth with good things; so that thy youth is renewed like the eagle's.*
- *God executeth righteousness and judgment for all that are oppressed.*
- *God made known his ways unto Moses, his acts unto the children of Israel.*

- *God is merciful and gracious, slow to anger, and plenteous in mercy.*
- *God will not always chide: neither will he keep his anger for ever.*
- *God hath not dealt with us after our sins; nor rewarded us according to our iniquities.*
- *For as the heaven is high above the earth, so great is his mercy toward them that fear him.*
- *As far as the east is from the west, so far hath he removed our transgressions from us.*
- *God, like as a father pitieth his children, so the LORD pitieth them that fear him.*
- *God knoweth our frame; he remembereth that we are dust.*
- *As for man, his days are as grass: as a flower of the field, so he flourisheth.*
- *For the wind passeth over it, and it is gone; and the place thereof shall know it no more.*
- *God's mercy is from everlasting to everlasting upon them that fear him, and his righteousness unto children's children;*
- *To such as keep his covenant, and to those that remember his commandments to do them.*
- *God hath prepared his throne in the heavens; and his kingdom ruleth over all **[Psalms 103]**.*

For each line, for each word, David could tell a very long story, a story of grace.

David ended his grace list by saying,

Bless the LORD, all his works in all places of his dominion: bless the LORD, O my soul.

We are all His works, we live in His dominion, and have all "benefitted" from His grace.

Paul to the Hebrews would say,

Neither is there any creature that is not manifest in his sight: but all things are *naked and opened unto the eyes of him with whom we have to do **[Hebrews 4:13]**.*

We are all creatures under grace.

This kind of grace, the Lord our God put it this way to Isaiah;

*It shall come to pass that before they call, I will answer; and while they are still speaking, I will hear **[Isaiah 65:24]**.*

This is communion with God above the mercy seat!

Before we call for forgiveness, we are already forgiven, before we call for healing, we are already healed, before we call for protection, we are already safe.

The Bible says a time shall come. I believe this is it – our time.

It is coming to pass, in this Jesus time. It is the time of grace and mercy.

David understood best that the Lord will not always blame, reproach or rebuke.

David had an experience of God's mercies when God sent Nathan to let him know God was not happy with what David had done to Uriah.

David did all in plain view of God, but God sent a story teller to talk to him.

When David repented of his sin, God accepted David back like all was and has always been well.

David, forgiven, lived and communed with God above the mercy seat.

He could then say,

*Give thanks unto the LORD, call upon his name, make known his deeds among the people **[1 Chronicles 16:8]**.*

God's throne is written grace all over it, and we need grace every time and in every space and place.

God Perfects

Paul to the Philippians says,

*Not that I have already obtained, or am already made perfect: but I press on, if so be that I may lay hold on that for which also I was laid hold on by Christ Jesus **[Philippians 3:12]**.*

This is where we are; trusting God for perfection.

We believe in God's saving grace, and build our faith in His word.

Even Paul needed God's assurance. He says to the Corinthians,

And he said unto me, My grace is sufficient for thee: for my strength is made perfect in weakness. Most gladly therefore will I rather glory in my infirmities, that the power of Christ may rest upon me **[2 Corinthians 12:9]**.

Isaiah will also speak,

³ Thou wilt keep him in perfect peace, whose mind is stayed on thee: because he trusteth in thee **[Isaiah 26:3]**.

It matters to God how we present ourselves to Him, yet we are never perfect. God will perfect, in His way.

Isaiah says we will hear a word behind us in our ears saying,

And thine ears shall hear a word behind thee, saying, This is the way, walk ye in it, when ye turn to the right hand, and when ye turn to the left **[Isaiah 30:21]**.

Isn't it interesting that Isaiah says a word and not a voice?

Yes, the Word of God will perfect us as we go.

Thank God for grace, for the Spirit of our God, whispers in our ears, in our hearts and captures our minds, so that we are perfected as we go.

The Bible says,

*³ For though we walk in the flesh, we do not war after the flesh:⁴ (For the weapons of our warfare are not carnal, but mighty through God to the pulling down of strong holds;)⁵ Casting down imaginations, and every high thing that exalteth itself against the knowledge of God, and bringing into captivity every thought to the obedience of Christ **[2 Corinthians 10:3-5]**.*

In any event, Jesus our Lord and Saviour says, *Take my yoke upon you, and learn of me; for I am meek and lowly in heart **[Mathew 11:29]**.*

We learn from the master.

Jesus did not beat the drums, yet all Jesus did was for the glory of the Father.

The glory and the beauty of God and Godliness was seen in what Jesus did and in how He did it.

We are children of God. We cannot be anything else, because God is our Father.

As John would say,

But as many as received him, to them gave he power to become the sons of God, even *to them that believe on his name [John1:12]* and,

Behold, what manner of love the Father hath bestowed upon us, that we should be called the sons of God [1 John 1:3].

Having been converted, David understood God's forgiveness and love.

David understood God creates.

David asks God to;

10 Create in me a clean heart, O God; and renew a right spirit within me. 11 Cast me not away from thy presence; and take not thy holy spirit from me. 12 Restore unto me the joy of thy salvation; and uphold me with thy free spirit [Psalms 51:10-12].

The Lord heard, the Lord answered.

Convinced and convicted, yet forgiven, David says,

⁴ One thing have I desired of the LORD, that will I seek after; that I may dwell in the house of the LORD all the days of my life, to behold the beauty of the LORD, and to enquire in his temple [Psalms 27:4].

Thank God for His grace, He does not deal with us as we deserve.

David had experienced the love and forgiveness of God.

David's son with Uriah's wife Bathsheba would be king of Judah after David's death.

That was grace.

As we walk this earth, those we meet on the way, should be convinced that they saw children of God.... as the building continues.

The story of David and that of Paul shows us the extent of God's love and forgiveness.

For Paul, it was the change that was instant and so powerful he literally flipped over, to an extent the Bible says,

*And the night following the Lord stood by him, and said, Be of good cheer, Paul: for as thou hast testified of me in Jerusalem, so must thou bear witness also at Rome **[Acts 23:11]**.*

Paul had changed. Paul was under God.

In Jerusalem, before the Jewish council, Paul gives an account of his encounter with Jesus. Paul says,

Brothers and fathers, listen now to my defense...."⁴ *I persecuted the followers of this Way to their death, arresting both men and women and throwing them into prison,* ⁵ *as the high priest and all the Council can themselves testify. I even obtained letters from them to their associates in Damascus, and went there to bring these people as prisoners to Jerusalem to be punished.*⁶ *"About noon as I came near Damascus, suddenly a bright light from heaven flashed around me.* ⁷ *I fell to the ground and heard a voice say to me, 'Saul! Saul! Why do you persecute me?'*⁸ *"'Who are you, Lord?' I asked." 'I am Jesus of Nazareth, whom you are persecuting,' he replied.* ⁹ *My companions saw the light, but they did not understand the voice of him who was speaking to me* **[Acts 22:1-8].**

The message of conversion, that time, during that incident, was strictly for Paul.

Those he had been travelling with never understood the voice they heard, but they saw what happened, the blindness.

Conversion takes understanding of God's love, His grace and the power of His might.

Paul's companions were the ones to assist him until Ananias, a Christian, prayed for him.

That was grace.

Paul, who used to get letters from Rome to persecute Christians, ended up before Caesar talking about this same Jesus.

The Bible says of Paul in Rome,

And when they had appointed him a day, there came many to him into his *lodging; to whom he expounded and testified the kingdom of God, persuading them concerning Jesus, both out of the law of Moses, and* out of *the prophets, from morning till evening.* **[Acts 28:23].**

As Jesus says,

My sheep hear my voice, and I know them, and they follow me **[John 10:27].**

Simply put, we are perfected by our God.

Manifestation Of The Holy Spirit

The Bible says,

⁸ And it came to pass, when Moses went out unto the tabernacle, that all the people rose up, and stood every man at his tent door, and looked after Moses, until he was gone into the tabernacle. ⁹ And it came to pass, as Moses entered into the tabernacle, the cloudy pillar *descended, and stood at the door of the tabernacle, and the Lord talked with Moses [**Exodus 33:8-9**].*

This is huge. The Lord did not speak to Moses, He spoke with Moses.

The Lord spoke to Moses in a cloudy pillar, in the Tabernacle of the congregation.

Moses spoke with God. No wonder the people stood at their doors.

The Bible says every man stood at his door; an unbelievable spectacle.

It was not a secret that God reasoned with Moses. The congregation saw what was happening.

I believe when the Lord our God shows up, there is no doubt that He did show up.

When the Bible says,

[10] And all the people saw the cloudy pillar stand at the tabernacle door: and all the people rose up and worshipped, every man in his tent door. [11] And the LORD spake unto Moses face to face, as a man speaketh unto his friend.

It cannot be any better. All the multitude of people saw.

When the Lord has worked on us, our actions, our language, our motives, everything, will shout out God's presence.

As the Bible says, Moses had been given a task, and Moses wanted to know who would be going with him. The Lord answered that question and also assured Moses;

^{14}My presence shall go with thee, and I will give thee rest [Exodus 33:14].

It is enough to have the presence of the Lord go with us.

The presence of the Lord with us makes the difference.

Moses knew that much.

Moses said if the presence of the Lord would not go with them, they Israel, was ordinary; fallible, insecure, exposed.

The Bible says of Moses communing with God,

And he said unto him, If thy presence go not with me, carry us not up hence. ^{16} For wherein shall it be known here that I and thy people have found grace in thy sight? is it not in that thou goest with us? so shall we be separated, I and thy people, from all the people that are upon the face of the earth [Exodus 33:15-16].

Moses knew, with God's presence, they were special, peculiar, chosen, royal.

This incident in the Bible is quite telling concerning God and His relationship with man.

Moses said to God; *[18]I beseech thee, shew me thy glory....*

The Lord God responded,

[20]Thou canst not see my face: for there shall no man see me, and live. [21] And the LORD said, Behold, there is a place by me, and thou shalt stand upon a rock: [22] And it shall come to pass, while my glory passeth by, that I will put thee in a clift of the rock, and will cover thee with my hand while I pass by: [23] And I will take away mine hand, and thou shalt see my back parts: but my face shall not be seen **[Exodus 33:18-23].**

Wow!

There was a place by the side of the Lord, where God could hide Moses, so that Moses would not die when he saw God!

Awesome!

The Bible says, *and he [Moses] was there with the LORD forty days and forty nights; he did neither eat bread, nor drink water* **[Exodus 34:28].**

Awesome.

*And when Aaron and all the children of Israel saw Moses, behold, the skin of his face shone; and they were afraid to come nigh him **[Exodus 33:30]**.*

God does not share His glory.

The Lord says,

*I am the LORD: that is my name: and my glory will I not give to another **[Isaiah 42:8]**.*

When Moses's face shown with the glory of God, that was grace.

We can also shine for our God, as long as we dwell in His presence.

When we have been with the Lord, all will see and know. Our faces, our being, will tell the story – that we had been with the Lord.

Holiness

The Lord our God has this to say;

*You are to be holy to me because I, the LORD, am holy, and I have set you apart from the nations to be my own **[Leviticus 20:26]***

I have always wondered how we can ever be holy, when the Bible says,

*Can the Ethiopian change his skin, or the leopard his spots? then may ye also do good, that are accustomed to do evil **[Jeremiah 13:23]**.*

This word to Jeremiah, meant for the children of Israel, means to me, we cannot do it on our own.

We can never be holy, unless the Lord makes us holy.

Then comes John, to reassure,

*As many as received him, to them gave he power to become the sons of God **[John 1:12]**.*

This is grace.

The Lord makes it possible – to be holy.

The Lord has given us weapons with which to fight this incessant war against evil.

The battles we fight every moment of time – for holiness.

Paul says,

[10] Finally, my brethren, be strong in the Lord, and in the power of his might.[11] Put on the whole armour of God, that ye may be able to stand against the wiles of the devil.[12] For we wrestle not against flesh and blood,

but against principalities, against powers, against the rulers of the darkness of this world, against spiritual wickedness in high places.[13] Wherefore take unto you the whole armour of God, that ye may be able to withstand in the evil day, and having done all, to stand.[14] Stand therefore, having your loins girt about with truth, and having on the breastplate of righteousness;[15] And your feet shod with the preparation of the gospel of peace;[16] Above all, taking the shield of faith, wherewith ye shall be able to quench all the fiery darts of the wicked.[17] And take the helmet of salvation, and the sword of the Spirit, which is the word of God:[18] Praying always with all prayer and supplication in the Spirit, and watching thereunto with all perseverance and supplication for all saints **[Ephesians 6:10-18].**

The Lord, indeed, made it possible, to be holy, for He wants us to abide in Him, and Him in us.

Abiding in God makes holiness possible.

The Bible says,

He who abides in Me, and I in him, bears much fruit; for without Me you can do nothing. 6 If anyone does not abide in Me, he is cast out as a branch and is withered; and they gather them and throw them into the fire, and they are burned. 7 If you abide in Me, and My words abide in you, you will ask what you desire, and it shall be done for you. 8 By this My Father is *glorified, that you bear much fruit; so you will be My disciples [**John 15:4-11**].*

This is awesome.

Abiding is accepting and acting in accordance with set rules.

This is too wonderful for me. Our God is faithful.

As we abide in Him, He abides in us. Powerful!

Abide, is dwelling in, remaining in, be present with, and being held and kept.

[Google definition]

Abiding addresses our posture and place.

We can abide in our God, as God avails Himself, for our habitation.

Wholesomeness comes with holiness.

Our Rear Guard

We have often talked about God as going before us.

Yes, He does. As Moses says,

*⁸The LORD himself goes before you and will be with you; he will never leave you nor forsake you. Do not be afraid; do not be discouraged [**Deuteronomy 31:8**].*

I have since realised, through the experiences of life, that we desperately need our rear covered.

The Lord our God knows we need both, that the Lord goes before us, and that the same God, covers our rear.

He says to the children of Israel,

*^{12} But you will not leave in haste or go in flight; for the LORD will go before you, the God of Israel will be your rear guard **[Isaiah 52:12]**.*

This is grace. We will not be running, we will walk, with our God.

Walking and running are completely different.

Walking gives the presence of peace, of comfort, walking means all is well.

Running is just the opposite. Running denotes fear, anxiety, and trouble.

The Lord says through the prophet Isaiah,

*Then your light will break forth like the dawn, and your healing will quickly appear; then your righteousness will go before you, and the glory of the LORD will be your rear guard **[Isaiah 58:8]**.*

This rear guard phenomenon was a puzzle until I realised, in life, it does not matter where you are and what you do, you need someone to cover your tracks, to cover your back.

In our lives, the Bible says the devil is like a roaring lion, seeking whom he may devour.

The lion habits have been extensively studied over time.

It is understood that the lion, in the jungle, has a very poor smell, by God's design.

The lion also has a very sharp eyesight or well developed night vision, also by God's design.

Google searches indicate the lion will follow behind, so softly another animal may not hear. It uses safe distance between prey and itself, until it is ready to attack. To ensure it is following correctly, it follows foot or paw prints.

Thank God for grace, human beings have very low level night vision.

In fact, human beings cannot see at night.

This is awesome, there are very few chances of human beings meeting or coming across the lion, as long as we, human beings, stay in our lane.

As long as we are in Jesus the Christ, the light of the world, we are safe.

In life, there are so many lions which attack from behind, if per adventure we go into the jungle, where the lion dwells.

We need a cover, one who can erase our foot prints so the enemy cannot see.

As the Bible says,

*⁸ Be sober, be vigilant; because your adversary the devil, as a roaring lion, walketh about, seeking whom he may devour [**1 Peter 5:8**].*

The Bible is clear – be sober. It is drunken people who go walk in darkness, where the enemy has the advantage of sight.

The devil is not in a hurry. The devil walks about. The devil uses stealth.

We need God to cover us, we need grace.

Most people can deal with what they are facing but many cannot deal with what is following them.

We say we can handle a situation, because, we say, we saw it coming.

Yes, by God's grace we can, as God gave us survival instincts.

What is behind you, you cannot see, because it is behind.

As I continued to search for more insights on lion behaviours, I established that hunting needs one to be very careful about wind direction.

God, by design, gave the lion a sharp sense of smell.

For cover, we need to check wind direction, to never go in the direction of the wind.

We have every reason to make God our hiding place, because the wind can change direction.

Let us hide behind the one who directs the wind.

We cannot afford to make it easy for the enemy.

As I was at pains to understand what Isaiah was saying about the rear guard, I accessed the following definition from Wikipedia;

"A rear-guard is that part of a military force that protects it from attack from the rear, either during an advance or withdrawal. The term can also be used to describe forces protecting lines, such as communication lines, behind an army. Even more generally, a rear-guard action may refer idiomatically to an attempt at preventing something though it is likely too late to be prevented; this idiomatic meaning may apply in either a military or non-military context.

Narrowly defined, a rear-guard is a covering detachment that protects the retreating main ground force element [main body], or column, and is charged with executing defensive or retrograde movements between the main body and the enemy to prevent the latter from attacking or interfering with the movement of the main body

[https://en.wikipedia.org/wiki/Rearguard
[Accessed 21/11/2018].

As I continued to read this article, I picked up the following:

1. It is a regular in wars to have a rear guard.
2. These troops protect the withdrawal of larger numbers of personnel [military or civilian] during a retreat.
3. The rear guard blocks, defends, delays, or interferes with advancing enemy forces.
4. The rear guard gives time to regroup and reorganize.
5. Rear-guard actions may be undertaken diverse ways.
6. Rear cover is concerned with defending strongpoints or tactically important terrain.
7. Rear cover may pre-emptively assault the enemy.
8. Rear cover gives time to prepare an own offensive operation.

9. The nature of combat in rear-guard actions involving combat between armies is typically desperate and vicious.
10. Rear-guard troops may incur heavy casualties.
11. Rear guard troops are required to sacrifice all of their combat strength and personnel for the benefit of the withdrawing forces.

This is grace, that we have our God, the Creator, as our rear guard.

In Psalms, the Bible says our God will send His angels to guard us.

Because thou hast made the LORD, which is my refuge, even the most High, thy habitation;[10] There shall no evil befall thee, neither shall any plague come nigh thy dwelling.[11] For he shall give his angels charge over thee, to keep thee in all thy ways ***[Psalms 91:9-11]***.

Christians are retreating from the armies of the enemy and through enemy territory.

This is double jeopardy. They need cover, which only God can give.

Retreat is not a negative. It is a strategy for survival.

Christians retreat into the hands of the Almighty, from the land of the enemy.

Regardless, retreating has costs.

When you retreat you leave everything behind. You run for dear life.

We leave everything behind, everything that detracts from the ultimate goal – holiness.

The old garments we leave behind. The old garments will sell us out.

We cannot retreat with any old identity.

We need camouflage that only God can give.

History records the story of retreat at the Battle of Dunkirk and the acknowledgement of a miracle [an against all odds event] that happened:

It is about the evacuation of Allied troops from Dunkirk, France in 1940, during the course of World War 2.

[The narration below is a direct quote from Wikipedia, with insignificant editions by the writer].

The morning of 1 June was clear–good flying weather, in contrast to the bad weather that had hindered air operations on 30 and 31 May [there were only two and a half good flying days in the whole operation]. Although Churchill had promised the French that the British would cover their escape, on the ground it was the French who held the line whilst the last remaining British soldiers were evacuated……..

The desperate resistance of Allied forces,.... had bought time for the evacuation of the bulk of the troops. The Germans captured some 35,000 soldiers..... These men had protected the evacuation until the last moment and were unable to embark.

The War Office made the decision to evacuate British forces on 25 May. In the nine days from 27 May–4 June, 338,226 men escaped, including 139,997 French, Polish, and Belgian troops, together with a small number of Dutch soldiers, aboard 861 vessels……..

The Royal Navy returned on 4 June, to rescue as many as possible of the French rear guard. Over 26,000 French soldiers were evacuated on that last day, but between 30,000 and 40,000 more were left behind and forced to surrender to the Germans.

The loss of material on the beaches was huge. The British Army left enough equipment behind to fit out about eight to ten divisions. Discarded in France were, among other things, huge supplies of ammunition, 880 field guns, 310 guns of large calibre, some 500 anti-aircraft guns, about 850 anti-tank guns, 11,000 machine guns, nearly 700 tanks, 20,000 motorcycles and 45,000 motor cars and lorries. Army equipment available at home was only just sufficient to equip two divisions. The British Army needed months to re-supply properly and some planned introductions of new equipment were halted while industrial resources concentrated on making good the losses. Officers told troops falling back from Dunkirk to burn or otherwise disable their trucks [so as not to let them benefit the advancing German forces] ....and it was obvious to many that God had answered the nation's collective prayer with the 'miracle of Dunkirk'. The evidence of God's intervention was clear for those who wished to see it....papers had written of calm seas [for those retreating] and the high mist which interfered with the accuracy of German bombers.

[https://en.wikipedia.org/wiki/Battle_of_Dunkirk
[Accessed November 21, 2018].

Thank God for His grace, He is our rear guard.

Retreating to God is grace.

The world as we know it is a maze. No one knows exactly what they ought to do and when.

It is grace that anyone can go through the day and get there - wherever.

It is grace that one can plan, work and breathe.

Everyone gets a chance to retreat, to turn back to God.

That chance to retreat is grace.

The Bible says, *if thou return to the Almighty, thou shalt be built up **[Job 22:23].***

The Lord is there before we get there.

God is Almighty; man is unpredictable, untrustworthy, inconsistent,

Moses says,

*The LORD your God which goeth before you, he shall fight for you, according to all that he did for you in Egypt before your eyes **[Deuteronomy 1:30]**.*

The Lord fights, for those that abide in Him.

The Lord is gracious, and still fights, for those that purport not to know God, giving them a chance to retreat.

When people walk drunk, the Lord gives opportunity for them to retreat, to turn back to God.

God will deliver, will rescue, so that one day we all talk the same - the story of God's grace.

The Lord says through Isaiah,

*I will go before thee, and make the crooked places straight: I will break in pieces the gates of brass, and cut in sunder the bars of iron **[Isaiah 45:2]**.*

There is no better story.

^{38} For the cloud of the LORD was upon the tabernacle by day, and fire was on it by night, in the sight of all

the house of Israel, throughout all their journeys [Exodus 40:38].

This God, who is Holy, who covers our rear, says to John;

[2] Unto the angel of the church of Ephesus write; These things saith he that holdeth the seven stars in his right hand, who walketh in the midst of the seven golden candlesticks;......

[8] And unto the angel of the church in Smyrna write; These things saith the first and the last, which was dead, and is alive...

[12] And to the angel of the church in Pergamos write; These things saith he which hath the sharp sword with two edges...

[18] And unto the angel of the church in Thyatira write; These things saith the Son of God, who hath his eyes like unto a flame of fire, and his feet are like fine brass;......

3 And unto the angel of the church in Sardis write; These things saith he that hath the seven Spirits of God, and the seven stars...

[7] And to the angel of the church in Philadelphia write; These things saith he that is holy, he that is true, he that hath the key of David, he that openeth, and no man shutteth; and shutteth, and no man openeth;....

*¹⁴ And unto the angel of the church of the Laodiceans write; These things saith the Amen, the faithful and true witness, the beginning of the creation of God **[Revelation chapters 2-3].***

These verses of Revelation say to me, God sustains.

As the Psalmist would say,

*By the word of the LORD were the heavens made; ..by the breath of his mouth...⁸ Let all the earth fear the LORD: let all the inhabitants of the world stand in awe of him.⁹ For he spake, and it was done; he commanded, and it stood fast **[Psalms 33:6-9].***

God is divine, and wants us divinely.

The Bible says,

*This is the covenant that I will make with them after those days, saith the Lord, I will put my laws into their hearts, and in their minds will I write them; 17 And their sins and iniquities will I remember no more **[Hebrews 10:16-26].***

That, is grace.

> ***Lord, I love the habitation of your house and the place where your glory dwells [Psalms 26:8].***

Grateful For Grace

CHAPTER 6

GREATER THAN THE TEMPLE

Solomon's Temple

According to the Hebrew Bible, Solomon's Temple, also known as the First Temple, was the Holy Temple in ancient Jerusalem before its destruction by Nebuchadnezzar II after the Siege of Jerusalem of 587 BCE and its subsequent replacement with the Second Temple in the 6th century BCE.

> Wikipedia.org. *[October 31, 2018] Solomon's Temple*
> *[Accessed November 23, 2018]*

Of this temple, the Bible says,

When Solomon had finished building the temple of the LORD ..... ² the LORD appeared to him a second time, as he had appeared to him at Gibeon.
³ The LORD said to him: "I have heard the prayer and plea you have made before me; I have consecrated this temple, which you have built, by putting my Name there forever. My eyes and my heart will always be there. ⁴ "As for you, if you walk before me faithfully with integrity of heart and uprightness,....I will establish your royal throne over Israel forever
[1 Kings 9:2-4].

After all the "effort" that went into the building of Solomon's temple, God saw it important to state to Solomon the true significance of the temple Solomon had just finished.

The Lord says even though my eyes will be on this temple, you need to walk in integrity and uprightness of heart, and then *I will establish your royal throne over Israel forever*.

The Lord is not mindful of the physical when the spiritual is in decay.

Yet building for God, in brick and mortar is a salvation issue.

The physical is and should be a ministration of the condition of the heart.

The temple that Solomon built, with all its splendour, could not save the children of Israel.

God sent the children of Israel into captivity whilst the temple was there. In the process, the temple was also destroyed, by fire.

Jesus then says of Himself,

*But I say unto you, that in this place is one greater than the temple **[Mathew 12:6]**.*

Yes, Jesus spoke and still speaks to the heart of every man.

Jesus Saves

Jesus was and is the Word of God, the Word that is quick and powerful, and the Word that is alive to our needs.

John says of Jesus;

*¹ In the beginning was the Word, and the Word was with God, and the Word was God.² The same was in the beginning with God.³ All things were made by him; and without him was not anything made that was made.⁴ In him was life; and the life was the light of men **[John 1:1-4]**.*

Paul also says of this Word, this Jesus;

¹² For the word of God is quick, and powerful, and sharper than any two-edged sword, piercing even to the dividing asunder of soul and spirit, and of the joints and marrow, and is a discerner of the thoughts and intents of the heart.¹³ Neither is there any creature that is not manifest in his sight: but all things are naked and opened unto the eyes of him with whom we have to do.¹⁴ Seeing then that we have a great high priest, that is passed into the heavens, Jesus the Son of God, let us hold fast our profession.¹⁵ For we have not an high priest which cannot be touched with the feeling of our infirmities; but was in all points tempted like as we are, yet without sin.¹⁶ Let us therefore come boldly unto the throne of grace, that we may obtain mercy, and find grace to help in time of need [Hebrews 4:12-16].

This same Word does not discriminate, for John also says:

^{12} But as many as received him, to them gave he power to become the sons of God, even to them that believe on his name [John 1:12].

Jesus ministers to our inner being. He ministers to our spirit.

Isaiah had said, of this Jesus,

6 For unto us a child is born, unto us a son is given: and the government shall be upon his shoulder: and his name shall be called Wonderful, Counsellor, The mighty God, The everlasting Father, The Prince of Peace. 7 Of the increase of his government and of peace there will be no end [Isaiah 9:6-7].

Jesus is the son of God, a son born to man for man's salvation.

A son born of God, to give to man what the temple Solomon built could not give.

The Bible says,

^{18} And Jesus came and spake unto them, saying, All power is given unto me in heaven and in earth.^{19} Go ye therefore, and teach all nations, baptizing them in the

name of the Father, and of the Son, and of the Holy Ghost:[20] *Teaching them to observe all things whatsoever I have commanded you: and, lo, I am with you always, even unto the end of the world* ***[Mathew 28:18-20]***.

Jesus has the power, and completely saves.

Paul had the ultimate experience of this power, on his way to Damascus and throughout all his journeys.

To the Hebrews he could then say of Jesus,

[25] *Wherefore he is able also to save them to the uttermost that come unto God by him, seeing he ever liveth to make intercession for them* ***[Hebrews 7:25]***.

For this reason, Paul says to the Romans,

[1] *I beseech you therefore, brethren, by the mercies of God, that ye present your bodies a living sacrifice, holy, acceptable unto God, which is your reasonable service* ***[Romans 12:1]***.

When God instructed the building of the sanctuary, it was and is not because God has nowhere to live or that God needs to hide.

This concept of the sanctuary I have alluded to earlier in this book [Chapter 5].

In essence, the sanctuary is God keeping presence of His law.

It was a grace issue.

As I understand this concept of the tabernacle Moses built, I surmise that God wanted man to remember, because man has a huge propensity to forget.

The children of Israel were asked by God to build Him a sanctuary that *they would carry* throughout their journeys, so that these "children" could remember.

The man mind is insignificant to understand God.

So building a physical structure for God does not give God credence, it just gives man an awareness of God.

When it comes to saving, to giving life, Jesus does.

The same applies to the churches we build for God, as much as it applies to the temple Solomon built.

The Bible says,

*Then the king commanded, and they quarried great stones, costly stones, to lay the foundation of the house with cut stones **[1 Kings 5:17]**.*

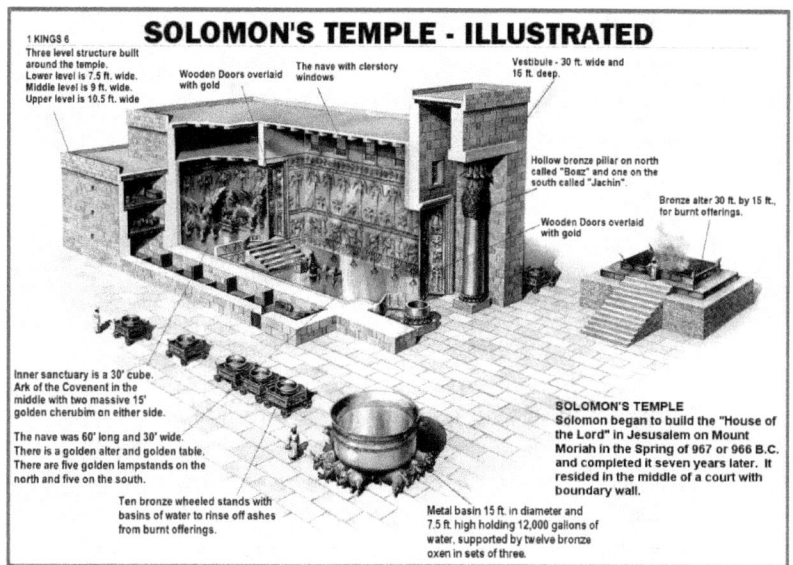

Solomon's Temple

https://freegracekids.com/2018/01/29/lesson-19-solomon-the-temple-and-sanctification/ [Accessed November 23, 2018]

The churches we build and the temple built all point us to God.

What we term building for God is only a manifestation of the relationship we have with our God.

To Solomon, the Lord God said, *⁶ but if you or your descendants turn away from me ....Israel will then become a byword and an object of ridicule among all peoples. ⁸ This temple will become a heap of rubble [1 Kings 9:6].*

Whilst the brick and mortar is good, the Lord our God wants us by Him and we want Him by us.

Regardless of the tabernacle and sanctuary that Moses built, Moses still wanted the glory of the Lord to go with them.

As I considered one of the discussions I found quite captivating in the Bible, the Lord said to Moses,

*^{14} My presence shall go with thee, and I will give thee rest.^{15} And he said unto him, If thy presence go not with me, carry us not up hence.^{16} For wherein shall it be known here that I and thy people have found grace in thy sight? is it not in that thou goest with us? so shall we be separated, I and thy people, from all the people that are upon the face of the earth.^{17} And the LORD said unto Moses, I will do this thing also that thou hast spoken: for thou hast found grace in my sight, and I know thee by name.^{18} And he said, I beseech thee, shew me thy glory.....^{21} And the LORD said, Behold, there is a place by me, and thou shalt stand upon a rock:^{22} And it shall come to pass, while my glory passeth by, that I will put thee in a clift of the rock, and will cover thee with my hand while I pass by **[Exodus 33:14-22].***

This was conspiracy, to save Moses. Jesus was the cleft of the rock. The rock that is higher than you and I.

The rock our Lord God takes us to, so that we may live, in His glory.

The Conspiracy Of Heaven

Paul encourages the Corinthians;

*Therefore, my beloved brethren, be ye stedfast, unmoveable, always abounding in the work of the Lord, forasmuch as ye know that your labour is not in vain in the Lord **[1 Corinthians 15:58]**.*

That steadfastness only comes when the law of God has found sanctuary in our hearts.

The Bible says,

*For Ezra had prepared his heart to seek the law of the LORD, and to do it, and to teach in Israel statutes and judgments **[Ezra 7:10]**.*

Ezra needed not to be pushed to do the law of the Lord, he purposed in his heart to do and to teach others of the same law.

Keeping, doing and teaching the law of the Lord by Ezra, was a precursor to the works done by Nehemiah in rebuilding the walls of Jerusalem.

Nehemiah would build on the fertile ground that Ezra had steadfastly worked on, to bring the hearts of the children of Israel back to their God.

Nehemiah would then say,

*And I arose in the night, I and some few men with me; neither told I any man what my God had put in my heart to do at Jerusalem: neither was there any beast with me, save the beast that I rode upon **[Nehemiah 2:12]**.*

Nehemiah was convinced by his God, of what he had to do in Jerusalem.

I found this verse quite fascinating when Nehemiah says *neither told I any man what my God had put in my heart to do*.

Building for God is a manifestation of a higher level relationship with the God you worship.

As Paul says,

*[19] Now therefore ye are no more strangers and foreigners, but fellow citizens with the saints, and of the household of God; [20] And are built upon the foundation of the apostles and prophets, Jesus Christ himself being the chief corner stone; [21] In whom all the building fitly framed together groweth unto an holy temple in the Lord: [22] In whom ye also are builded together for an habitation of God through the Spirit **[Ephesians 2:19-22]**.*

Heaven was in collusion, God the Father, God the Son and God the Holy Spirit.

Peter says it in his own way;

*Ye also, as lively stones, are built up a spiritual house acceptable to God by Jesus Christ [**1 Peter 2:5**].*

God watches over the building of His house.

The Bible says,

*[11] And the word of the LORD came to Solomon, saying, [12] Concerning this house which thou art in building, if thou wilt walk in my statutes, and execute my judgments, and keep all my commandments to walk in them; then will I perform my word with thee [**1 Kings 6:11-12**].*

The temple was the means to get man back to God.

Solomon prays,

*LORD, the God of Israel, there is no God like you in heaven above or on earth below—you who keep your covenant of love with your servants who continue wholeheartedly in your way [**1 Kings 8:22**].*

Solomon recognized the brick and mortar temple was good, to and for them that wholeheartedly sought the face of the Lord.

Solomon says, *with your mouth you have promised and with your hand you have fulfilled it [**1 Kings 8:24**].*

This is our God, this is grace.

As Paul says,

*For it is God who works in you both to will and to do for His good pleasure **[Philippians 2:13]**.*

It does not matter what and how we do what we do, it is grace through and through, as children of God.

The Bible says,

*Now when Solomon had made an end of praying, the fire came down from heaven, and consumed the burnt offering and the sacrifices; and the glory of the LORD filled the house. ² And the priests could not enter into the house of the LORD, because the glory of the LORD had filled the LORD's house **[2 Chronicles 7]**.*

Jesus is greater than the temple.

The Bible says, *for the LORD your God is a consuming fire, a jealous God **[Deuteronomy 4:24]**.*

As God the Father and His son Jesus are one, Jesus came down to fill up Solomon's temple.

When He did, the priests could not enter. Someone greater, had come down. Someone greater, had taken residence.

At the end of it all, it was never Solomon's temple; it was the Lord's house.

Grateful For Grace

As God's glory filled the brick and mortar temple, His glory also fills this, me and you, flesh and blood temple, for we are God's temple.

As Paul would say, again to the Corinthians,

19 Do you not know that your bodies are temples of the Holy Spirit, who is in you, whom you have received from God? You are not your own; 20 you were bought at a price. Therefore honor God with your bodies ***[1 Corinthians 6:19-20].***

Again Paul says,

To them God would make known what are the riches of the glory of this mystery among the Gentiles, which is Christ in you, the hope of glory ***[Colossians 1:27].***

What grace?

When the Lord fills His temple, this body temple, no one can enter. Hell cannot prevail against us!

This grace, is amazing.

As Jesus Himself said, as much as He said it to Peter,

And I say also unto thee, That thou art Peter, and upon this rock I will build my church; and the gates of hell shall not prevail against it ***[Matthew 16:18].***

This is where we stand; this is where we sit, on Christ the solid rock.

The temple Solomon built, was a perfect reminder of the tabernacle Moses built.

The Bible says,

³ And when all the children of Israel saw how the fire came down, and the glory of the LORD upon the house, they bowed themselves with their faces to the ground upon the pavement, and worshipped, and praised the LORD, saying, For he is good; for his mercy endureth forever **[2 Chronicles 7:3]**.

Paul would say,

Our fathers had the tabernacle of witness in the wilderness, as he had appointed, speaking unto Moses, that he should make it according to the fashion that he had seen. ⁴⁸ Howbeit the most High dwelleth not in temples made with hands; as saith the prophet, ⁴⁹ Heaven is my throne, and earth is my footstool: what house will ye build me? saith the Lord: or what is the place of my rest? ⁵⁰ Hath not my hand made all these things **[Acts 7:44]**.

The Lord God made them all, the temple that Solomon built, and the tabernacle that Moses built.
Both were witnesses, that the Lord God loves His own, those that love and diligently seek Him, with all their hearts.

The temple gives hope.

*Thus saith the LORD, The heaven is my throne, and the earth is my footstool: where is the house that ye build unto me? and where is the place of my rest? ² For all those things hath mine hand made, and all those things have been, saith the LORD: but to this man will I look, even to him that is poor and of a contrite spirit, and trembleth at my word **[Isaiah 66:1]**.*

The same the Lord desires of us, that as we hope in our God, we also trust hoped and depend on the oracles of God.

Assurance

After the building of the brick and mortar temple, the Lord God visited Solomon;

*¹² And the LORD appeared to Solomon by night, and said unto him, I have heard thy prayer, and have chosen this place to myself for an house of sacrifice **[2 Chronicles 7]**.*

Equally so, after Paul's conversion and his many errands for God, the Bible says,

*And the night following the Lord stood by him, and said, Be of good cheer, Paul: for as thou hast testified of me in Jerusalem, so must thou bear witness also at Rome **[Acts 23:11]**.*

To God, the body temple is greater than "Solomon's" temple.

Building for God, in the spiritual and in the physical, is just our way of saying God is with us.

Faithful God

God says to Solomon, when things are not good, come to this temple and pray.

This says to me, yes, Solomon's temple was the house of God, the house of prayer for all people, but hey, when things go wrong, this house is for us too.

The Lord says,

*If I shut up heaven that there be no rain, or if I command the locusts to devour the land, or if I send pestilence among my people **[2 Chronicles 7:13]**.*

God would bless in the temple, He would deliver in the temple, and God would heal in the temple.

The Lord says in :*^{14} If my people, which are called by my name, shall humble themselves, and pray, and seek my face, and turn from their wicked ways; then will I hear from heaven, and will forgive their sin, and will heal their land **[2 Chronicles 7:14]**.*

Our God has done it all, so that we can have it all, in Jesus, our Lord and Saviour.

The Challenges

The challenges in building are many. It does not matter the material, brick and mortar or flesh and blood,

Building is a challenge.

During the reconstruction work in Nehemiah's time, the Bible says,

*And Judah said, The strength of the bearers of burdens is decayed, and there is much rubbish; so that we are not able to build the wall **[Nehemiah 4:10]**.*

As alluded to in the introduction of this book, we are all construction sites.

Building hazards on a construction site saps all the energy, and rubbish is plenty.

That rubbish, everyone comes across it in life, in one way or the other.

It is that something which takes your strength away.

Each day, each week, each month, each year, has its own rubbish.

It is grace that gives us power and energy to keep going, keep trusting, and keep believing.

It is God.

The challenges are not just inward, in Judah, they are also outside of us.

The Bible says,

Now when the adversaries of Judah and Benjamin heard that the children of the captivity builded the temple unto the LORD God of Israel; ^{2} Then they came to Zerubbabel, and to the chief of the fathers, and said unto them, Let us build with you: for we seek your God, as ye do; and we do sacrifice unto him ....^{3} But Zerubbabel, and Jeshua, and the rest of the chief of the fathers of Israel, said unto them, Ye have nothing to do with us to build an house unto our God; but we ourselves together will build unto the LORD God..... ^{4} Then the people of the land weakened the hands of the people of Judah, and troubled them in building [Ezra 4:1-4].

This challenge is huge.

There is always an enemy within; people who purport to be on our side, when the intention is to weaken us or change our focus.

Building is a grace demanding situation.

The paths of this world have thorns and thistles, rocks and stones, deserts and valleys, hills and mountains, scorpions and snakes.

We need God. We need grace.

The seemingly good place is full of people who will say *Let us build with you: for we seek your God, as ye do,* when they really mean for us to fall out of favour with our God.

To know how to answer is grace. The Bible says,

*Let your speech be always with grace, seasoned with salt, that ye may know how ye ought to answer every man **[Colossians 4:6].***

There will be challenges in life. Challenges in building, but grace sustain.

The temple that endures is you and I.

We are the house of God.

The Lord says to Solomon, if you should falter, I will cut you out, both you and the temple, regardless of the magnificence of the temple you built, and

*All who pass by will be appalled and will scoff and say, 'Why has the LORD done such a thing to this land and to this temple?' ⁹ People will answer, 'Because they have forsaken the LORD their God...that is why the LORD brought all this disaster on them **[2 Chronicles 7:8-9]**.*

Because Jesus is greater than the temple that Solomon built, we are covered, for built on Jesus and by Jesus, the gates of hell cannot prevail against us.

Even when we falter, our God is faithful. He says *if* we return, He is waiting; to bless, to deliver, to restore, to heal.

To our God, we are His little children, still growing in the knowledge of God.

The Bible then says,

Ye are of God, little children, and have overcome them: because greater is he that is in you, than he that is in the world ***[1 John 4:4].***

Jesus, in us, is our hope and our glory.

To them God has chosen to make known among the Gentiles the glorious riches of this mystery, which is Christ in you, the hope of glory ***[Colossians 1:27].***

This is the conspiracy of heaven. This is grace.

> ***Lord, I love the habitation of your house and the place where your glory dwells [Psalms 26:8].***

CHAPTER 7

THE SAFETY NET

Grace Coated

Ultimately, the mind, power and grace of God is in everything that is man and concerns man.

- God is in the rains, the thunderstorms and the lightning of our lives.
- He is in the poverty and the famine; He is in the laughter too.
- God is in the crying and the anxiety, He is in the riches, the peace and the comfort.
- God is in the panic and the fear; He is in the mudslides and the floods too.
- God is in the blindness and the leprosy; He is in the darkness and the light too.

David says,

Lord, who shall abide in thy tabernacle? Who shall dwell in thy holy hill? ***[Psalm 15:1].***

To see thy power and thy glory, so as I have seen thee in the sanctuary ***[Psalm 63:2].***

In the tabernacle our struggles are grace coated.

There are issues of life that David did not understand.

He says I understood when I went into the sanctuary of God.

He says,

*^{16} When I thought to know this, it was too painful for me; ^{17} until I went into the sanctuary of God; then understood I their end **[Psalm 73:16-17]**.*

The confusion we get as we deal man to man is huge.

David, in his greatness, was as challenged as any one of us.

Some issues, some situations, some circumstances, some relationships, are just painful.

We can only understand the issues of life when we dwell in the presence of the Lord.

David says,

*Thou shalt hide them in the secret of thy presence from the pride of man: thou shalt keep them secretly in a pavilion from the strife of tongues **[Psalm 31:20]**.*

The pride of man is huge, and so is the strife that a tongue can bring.

We are only hid from the wrath of such, in the temple of the Lord, in God's house, in God.

We run to God and hide.

As I considered life, as I know and understand life, I got three issues or challenges that we face as human beings, which should force us to run to God and hide.

Fear

Moses says, *the eternal God is thy refuge, and underneath are the everlasting arms: and he shall thrust out the enemy from before thee **[Deuteronomy 33:27]**.*

Fear is debilitating.

Fear incapacitates.

Fear takes away all energy, it drains dry.

Fear weakens resolve, it is unbearable.

Fear removes focus on God, it takes away faith.

Fear paralyses both the body and the will.

Fear leads to disconnect with Godly principles.

David says,

*[4] I sought the LORD, and he heard me, and delivered me from all my fears **[Psalms 34]**.*

David too was afraid.

This was a man whom God could count on. He was solid against the lions, against the hyenas, against Goliath, but there were times when he was *sore afraid*. David was *painfully afraid*.

Not once, not twice, but many times.

This was a man God had raised.

As Paul quotes scripture and says,

*And when he had removed him [Saul removed], he [God] raised up unto them David to be their king; to whom also he gave their testimony, and said, I have found David the son of Jesse, a man after mine own heart, which shall fulfil all my will **[Acts13:22]**.*

Even this man David, as described by Paul, was afraid.

Fear drives most of what we do as people.

Fear of darkness, fear of the future, fear of the unknown.

Fear does not respect, kings and queens, boy or girl, man or woman.

We are all fearful, in time, in place and in space.

The Bible says, [2] *and David laid up these words in his heart, and was sore afraid of Achish the king of Gath **[1 Samuel 21:12]**.*

The Bible is saying, even people after God's heart will be afraid.

The word sore means pain and discomfort. This means David was painfully afraid of the king of Gath.

That fear was real. Gath was the place David fled to when he was fleeing from Saul *[I Samuel21:10].*

David was sore afraid because he did not know what the king of Gath would do.

Not knowing is painful.

David was afraid of God too. The Bible says,

*And David was afraid of the LORD that day, and said, How shall the ark of the LORD come to me?[**2 Samuel 6:9].***

Thank God David had a mind to go to the Lord's tabernacle.

David later says,

*Thou art my hiding place [Lord]; thou shalt preserve me from trouble; thou shalt compass me about with songs of deliverance **[Psalms 32:7].***

When afraid, the Lord God is our hiding place, our tabernacle, and our habitation.

After the event, David says,

*The angel of the LORD encampeth round about them that fear him, and delivereth them **[Psalms 34:7]**.*

When you have been delivered you know it.

You may not talk about it but all of you will say, *O taste and see that the Lord is good **[Psalms 34:8]**.*

David is not confused.

He says, *⁹ O fear the LORD, ye his saints: for there is no want to them that fear him **[Psalms 34:9]**.*

Those who have gone through what they have gone through, of life, will testify. They will tell their story, of grace.

God is our safety net, God is the safety net.

After all the running that David did in his life, he says,

*God is our refuge and strength, a very present help in trouble **[Psalm 46:1]**.*

Abraham too was fearful, not every time, but sometimes.

This was a man in whom God had imputed righteousness because he [Abraham] had believed God.

This is captured by James where the Bible says,

*And the scripture was fulfilled which saith, Abraham believed God, and it was imputed unto him for righteousness: and he was called the Friend of God **[James 2:23]**.*

Still, when fear strikes, only firm faith in the Lord God reassures.

The Bible says,

*After these things the word of the LORD came unto Abram in a vision, saying, Fear not, Abram: I am thy shield, and thy exceeding great reward **[Genesis 15:1]**.*

Abraham was afraid.

Chapter 14 of Genesis was a war chapter, things were not ok, and Abraham had reason to be afraid.

With three hundred and eighteen men, there was no way Abraham could have defeated the armies of five kings.

The Bible says Abraham's servants were trained in war. It was not physical war, not bows and spears, it was spiritual war.

In the realms of the physical, a little over three hundred men would not match the enemy from five kingdoms.

Abrahams's servants had been trained to rely on God, the Creator of the Universe, the Giver of Life.

This is awesome.

These servants knew who fought on their side. The numbers did not matter!

Only God gives victory.

Abraham went to war with three hundred and eighteen men because he knew where he stood, and how he was going to stand.

Abraham had favour from God. It was grace.

Abraham knew who was on his side, who fought his battles, who gave victory.

It could never be three hundred men without God. It had to be three hundred men with God.

The three hundred men had to tell the story. They were just witnesses.

This battle was fought by God, with three hundred witnesses in tow!

Gideon must have also remembered this when he went to fight the Midianites.

Three hundred men – does God love three hundred?

Gideon conquered and plundered, with three hundred men.

The Bible says,

*And the Midianites and the Amalekites and all the children of the east lay along in the valley like grasshoppers for multitude; and their camels were without number, as the sand by the sea side for multitude **[Judges 7:12]**.*

Gideon's men fought and conquered, not because they were good; that they could lap river water like dogs.

Gideon's man fought and conquered, because the Lord God rode on their banner.

Gideon's men were not good enough for God to work with, but they were good enough witnesses!

As Moses said, they were different, because the Lord God went before them.

In the book of Isaiah, the Lord says,

*But now, thus says the LORD, who created you, O Jacob, And He who formed you, O Israel: Fear not, for I have redeemed you; I have called you by your name; You are Mine **[Isaiah 43:1]**.*

Our God reassures.

Poverty and Famine

Poverty and famine go together.

In Ethiopia, in South America, in India, in Yemen, in

Nepal, poverty and famine know no limits.

E. Vuong. [July 11, 2014]Measuring Global Poverty.
[Accessed November 29, 2018]

Poverty and famine are not just physical. Famine and poverty have very simple definitions – lack.

Even to the children of Israel, the chosen tribes, poverty and famine were reported.

Not by man but by God.

The Bible talks about the siege of Samaria and how bad the famine was in ***2 Kings 6:25***.

The Bible says famine in Israel forced Jacob and his family to seek solace in Egypt.

Poverty and famine forced Naomi and her family to go to Moab.

Poverty is not good.

A. Porter [April 5, 2017] *Extreme poverty set to rise across Southern Africa* **[Accessed November 29, 2018]**

Poverty consumes. Poverty and famine deprives the mind of good judgement.

Thank God He is in the poverty and the famine too.

For Jacob, God prepared Joseph. For Naomi, God prepared Ruth and Boaz.

David says,

Behold, the eye of the LORD *is upon them that fear him, upon them that hope in his mercy; [19] To deliver their soul from death, and to keep them alive in famine* ***[Psalm 33:18-19].***

The prophet Isaiah says of God for those in need, for those who lack,

*For thou hast been a strength to the poor, a strength to the needy in his distress, a refuge from the storm, a shadow from the heat, when the blast of the terrible ones is as a storm against the wall **[Isaiah 25:4]**.*

This is the magnificence of God. This is grace.

Disease

Of the many definitions of disease, such as illness or sickness, I found malady very interesting.

Malady, amongst its many definitions such as illness and sickness, it also includes disorder, condition, problem or difficulty.

Maladies we encounter every other day of our lives.

The Psalmist says, *He sent his word, and healed them, and delivered them from their destructions **[Psalms 107:20]**.*

Jesus, as reported by Luke, and quoting from the book of Isaiah says,

The Spirit of the Lord is upon me, because he hath anointed me to preach the gospel to the poor; he hath sent me to heal the broken-hearted, to preach

*deliverance to the captives, and recovering of sight to the blind, to set at liberty them that are bruised **[Luke 4:18-20]**.*

This is the condition of man, regardless of education, political affiliation, regardless of anything.

Jesus truly saves.

Jesus delivers, from all our maladies.

Jesus is our safety net.

That, is grace.

> ***Lord, I love the habitation of your house and the place where your glory dwells [Psalms 26:8].***

CHAPTER 8

THE BALM OF GILEAD

The Great Physician

God heals. It is not the medicine or the integrity of the doctors.

The prophet Jeremiah made reference to the balm of Gilead in two passages of the Bible:

The Bible says,

Is there no balm in Gilead; is there no physician there? why then is not the health of the daughter of my people recovered [Jeremiah 8:22].

Jeremiah further prescribes,

Go up into Gilead, and take balm, O virgin, the daughter of Egypt: in vain shalt thou use many medicines; for thou shalt not be cured [Jeremiah 46:11].

The disease Jeremiah is referring to is beyond the physical.

The disease Jeremiah mentions is spiritual decay.

He is wondering what has become of the children of God.

How come they keep sinning, he is asking.

The Bible says Jeremiah would stand and exhort the people to go back to God, but they would not.

They had sought many solutions, many medicines he says, but no joy, no healing, no restoration.

Jeremiah starts by wondering why the daughter has not been to Gilead, and then he commands that she goes to Gilead.

Jeremiah understood the situation that the daughter was in, but she did not.

Jeremiah knew this daughter needed someone to give the directions.

If Jeremiah had lived in our day, where he put Gilead, he would have put Jesus.

Jesus is not an alternative; He is the first and only, the first and last choice.

Jesus is the great physician.

He knows *all* our situations and circumstances, both in time and place.

Jeremiah says,

*Babylon is suddenly fallen and destroyed: howl for her; take balm for her pain, if so be she may be healed [**Jeremiah 51:8**].*

It does not matter what man call you, Babylon or Israel, we all need healing.

The medicine is the same, it is the balm of Gilead, and it is Jesus.

An interesting passage of the Bible reads,

*And the men which were expressed by name rose up, and took the captives, and with the spoil clothed all that were naked among them, and arrayed them, and shod them, and gave them to eat and to drink, and anointed them, and carried all the feeble of them upon asses, and brought them to Jericho, the city of palm trees, to their brethren: then they returned to Samaria [**2 Chronicles 28:15**].*

A situation had come up.

The tribes of Israel fought against each other and against foreign legions.

One part beat the other and took spoil and people to Samaria.

The Lord, ever merciful, made sure His prophet, Oded was on hand.

Even when we fight each other, we need to always come back and bandage one another.

After cleaning the wounds we caused, we need to take our own to their place, a place of refuge, and a place of healing, their Jericho, a city of palm trees.

Palm trees meant perennial peace, meant victory, meant fertility.

Beaten up by the enemy, in God we would be whole again, we would be productive again, we would be evergreen again.

This is how our God so cares for us.

In disobedience to God, our God can discipline. He will wound, but He will restore.

^{39} See now that I, even I, am he, and there is no god with me: I kill, and I make alive; I wound, and I heal: neither is there any that can deliver out of my hand [Deuteronomy 32:29].

This is grace.

It does not matter what we have done, in His correction, God is ever so full of grace and mercy.

This balm is tradable.

When we have lost ourselves in the maze of this life, we ought to remember to take a little balm, that's the present we can give to posterity.

The Bible says,

And their father Israel said unto them, If it must be so now, do this; take of the best fruits in the land in your vessels, and carry down the man a present, a little balm, and a little honey, spices, and myrrh, nuts, and almonds [Genesis 43:11].

Is it not surprising, that in Gilead stayed the grand children of Ishmael.

We talk Isaac, but yes, Ishmael was loved and cared for by God.

Even to Ishmael, take a little balm.

The balm heals broken relationships.

Ishmael will appreciate, that even though the balm came from where he stays, a little balm from you is good, it makes all the difference.

This is God's doing.

And they sat down to eat bread: and they lifted up their eyes and looked, and, behold, a company of

Ishmaelites came from Gilead with their camels bearing spicery and balm and myrrh, going to carry it down to Egypt [Genesis 37:25].

To Tyrus the Lord says,

Judah, and the land of Israel, they were thy merchants: they traded in thy… and balm [Ezekiel 27:17].

This Lord sent a word of caution to a city that knew there was balm around but never appreciated it.

They knew God but were never part of God or Godliness.

If the medicine is not taken, the healing will not take place.

Perhaps that is why Jeremiah was wondering why the daughter of Zion had not been healed.

Some refuse the medicine because the Ishmaelite brought it. Some feel they just do not need it, let alone want it. Some buy it as an item of trade but never hold its value.

The balm of Gilead is our God. He says, *for I am the Lord that healeth thee [Exodus 15:26-27].*

Outside God, there is no healing.

Leprosy and Blindness

As I was considering what we call disease, I considered the two diseases called leprosy and blindness are not "ordinary" diseases.

I therefore decided to give these two diseases their own space.

Disease does not discriminate. Disease makes us all mere mortals.

Disease invades from the inside out, from army generals to servants, from the learned to the illiterate, from the rich to the poor.

There are two diseases that the Bible talks of more than any other.

Leprosy

The Bible says, *And there came a leper to him, beseeching him, and kneeling down to him, and saying unto him, If thou wilt, thou canst make me clean.* ^{41} *And Jesus, moved with compassion, put forth his hand, and touched him, and saith unto him, I will; be thou clean.* ^{42} *And as soon as he had spoken, immediately the leprosy departed from him, and he was cleansed **[Mark 1:40-42/Matthew 8:1-4/Luke 5:13]**.*

The leper came to Christ, not because Christ did not know him or see him.

Jesus deliberately passed by the leper. Jesus was pitiful.

As David says,

Like as a father pitieth his children, so the LORD pitieth them that fear him. [14] For he knoweth our frame; he remembereth that we are dust [Psalms 103:13].

Jesus does not play dice with the lives of man, He wants man to relate.

The leper had a choice, to respond or to keep quiet.

When you have leprosy, you need someone who remembers you.

The everyday practice is all persons with leprosy are outcasts.

These are the people who need help most, simply because they are incapacitated by leprosy. Yet they are to stay outside the camp.

The Bible again says about these out casts,

And as he entered into a certain village, there met him ten men that were lepers, which stood afar off: [13] And they lifted up their voices, and said, Jesus, Master, have mercy on us. ⁱ⁴ *And when he saw them, he said unto them, Go shew yourselves unto the priests. And it came to pass, that, as they went, they were cleansed* **[Luke 17:12-14].**

This is leprosy.

You could not meet a leprosy ravaged man on any village path.

Men with leprosy removed themselves from the paths of the good.

Jesus knew of these ten men. He is in the leprosy too.

He went closer to them; Jesus made it easier for the outcasts to see Him.

Jesus already knew, He had already heard.

This is God.

He knows the feeling of our infirmities.

Jesus knows how leprosy hurts, he knows the disfigurement, He knows the reproach that is thrown at the sick, not with any other disease, but with leprosy.

Jesus knows.

God knows leprosy does not need healing, it needs cleansing.

Healing is for wounds, cleansing is for the inner man, the heart, the mind.

Jesus knows man more than man knows himself.

Jesus needed to give instruction - go and show yourselves to the priest.

That was a test of faith. That was all the lepers needed to do, and that is all we need to do.

We need to go and show ourselves to the High Priest.

Jesus is the High Priest.

Thank God for Jesus. Jesus does not wait for us to get there, He heals, He cleanses as soon as we start moving, going back to the priest who declared us unclean in the first place.

That is grace.

This story told by one who had leprosy is huge. The story begins by defining the disease:

*And the plague in sight be [if] deeper than the skin of his flesh, it is a plague of leprosy **[Leviticus 13:3]**.*

Leprosy is deeper than the skin.

People with leprosy do not belong; they are condemned by the disease.

As indicated in chapter 1, a building condemned is no longer of any use; it is due for pulling down.

Not so with Jesus, not so with our God. Jesus went to the cross to rescue the condemned.

The story continues - *And there were four leprous men at the entering in of the gate: and they said one to another, Why sit we here until we die? ⁴ If we say, We will enter into the city, then the famine is in the city, and we shall die there: and if we sit still here, we die also. Now therefore come, and let us fall unto the host of the Syrians: if they save us alive, we shall live; and if they kill us, we shall but die **[2 Kings 7:3-4]**.*

Outcasts can still think and make very bold decisions.

Outcasts talk to each other, they ask the right questions; *why are we sitting here?*

Every man has leprosy of some sort.

To recognise exactly what the stakes are that are against you, and move, is grace.

Where leprosy is concerned, the instructions are clear:

The Bible says,

*And the LORD spake unto Moses, saying, ² Command the children of Israel, that they put out of the camp every leper, and every one that hath an issue, and whosoever is defiled by the dead: ³ Both male and female shall ye put out, without the camp shall ye put them; that they defile not their camps, in the midst whereof I dwell **[Numbers 5:1-3]**.*

Grace is not delayed and cannot be delayed.

Miriam too had leprosy *[Numbers 12:1-14]*.

Miriam found grace when Moses prayed for her and pleaded with God to heal her.

Miriam found grace – she had leprosy for only seven days.

But Uzziah died a leper, because leprosy cuts people from the house of the Lord.

The Bible says,

Then Uzziah was angry with the priests, [and] the leprosy even rose up in his forehead before the priests in the house of the LORD, ...²⁰ And Azariah the chief priest, and all the priests, looked upon him, and, behold, he was leprous in his forehead, and they thrust him out from thence; yea, himself hasted also to go out, *because the LORD had smitten him. ^{21} And Uzziah the king was a leper unto the day of his death, and dwelt in a several house, being a leper; for he was cut off from the house of the LORD [2 Chronicles 26:19].*

Leprosy rose whilst a king was in the house of the Lord!

How so?

When one is off he is off. It does not matter where they stand or who they are.

If we do not turn back to God we will die of leprosy, yet God is so ready to forgive, heal and cleanse.

Uzziah hasted to go out of God's house, when he saw that he had leprosy, moving further away from God.

The leprosy Uzziah had started in his forehead, in his mind, in his head, in his heart.

The priests could only see it when it was on his forehead.

Leprosy can define your social, spiritual, physical or mental state. Leprosy can cover every part of the human being.

It is a mystery of Godliness that leprosy is declared clean when the whole body turns white, when the whiteness should have covered the whole body [*Leviticus chapter 13].*

To me, this is restoration. This is grace.

Only God makes white, whether white as snow or white as sheep's wool, but it is white.

When leprosy is healed, man is new, fresh, uncontaminated, yet that man will be coming from outside the camp.

Outside the camp is dirty, but even from there, the Lord will make white.

The conversation between Moses and his God is quite interesting.

The Lord says to Moses, for proof that I have sent you, use a leprosy stunt will do;

That they may believe that the LORD God of their fathers, the God of Abraham, the God of Isaac, and the God of Jacob, hath appeared unto thee. ⁶ And the LORD said furthermore unto him, Put now thine hand into thy bosom. And he put his hand into his bosom: and when he took it out, behold, his hand was leprous as snow. ⁷ And he said, Put thine hand into thy bosom again. And he put his hand into his bosom again; and plucked it out of his bosom, and, behold, it was turned again as his other flesh. ⁸ And it shall come *to pass, if they will not believe thee, neither hearken to the voice of the first sign, that they will believe the voice of the latter sign [Exodus 4:5-8].*

The first sign was the rod changed into a serpent and then a rod again.

God says, if the children of Israel fail to believe when you cast the rod down and it turns into a serpent, then you hold its tail, you pick it up and it turns into a rod again, don't worry. When that happens, and they fail to believe, do this second one?

This second one, they will believe, the leprosy act.

The Lord is saying there is a miracle in leprosy healed.

When God is not in it there is no healing, there is no cleansing.

The sceptics will believe when someone has been cleansed of leprosy!

The healing, the cleansing is ours.

The Bible says,

But if we walk in the light, as he is in the light, we have fellowship one with another, and the blood of Jesus Christ his Son cleanseth us from all sin [1 John 1:7].

Naaman was cleansed.

Naaman's story is a story of belief, of trust, of faith in the face of leprosy.

The Lord God, led Naaman to the Jordan river.

¹⁰ And Elisha sent a messenger unto him, saying, Go and wash in Jordan seven times, and thy flesh shall come again to thee, and thou shalt be clean..... ¹¹ But Naaman was wroth.... and said.. I thought, He will surely come out to me, and stand, and call on the name of the LORD his God, and strike his hand over the place, and recover the leper. ¹² Are not Abana and Pharpar, rivers of Damascus, better than all the waters of Israel? may I not wash in them, and be clean? **[2 Kings 5:10-12].**

Elisha just thought to let Naaman know, God's ways are not our ways.

God's ways can make the proud and powerful angry, but God is God.

You cannot mark God, you cannot judge God. You cannot tell God. He will do what He does, the way He does it.

What rivers? Elisha could have asked.

I always think, if God had decided it that way, Naaman would have gone back to see the rivers he so loved dry.

Abana and Pharpar do not matter.

The healing is not in the rivers, it is in God and from God.

[13] And his servants came near, and spake unto him, and said, My father, if the prophet had bid thee do some great thing, wouldest thou not have done it? how much rather then, when he saith to thee, Wash, and be clean?

Naaman was a man of valour, but when it came to Godly things, the maids, the armour bearers, the escorts, the servants, were more receptive.

They understood better. They took and take God at His word. They reason with God better. They just know there is a prophet in Samaria; they just know the Lord said, and to them, that is enough.

[14] Then went he down, and dipped himself seven times in Jordan, according to the saying of the man of God: and his flesh came again like unto the flesh of a little child, and he was clean.

Obedience matters.

This God, is merciful.

He is the most merciful Father. Our balm of Gilead.

[15] And he returned to the man of God, he and all his company, and came, and stood before him: and he said, Behold, now I know that there is no God in all the earth, but in Israel:

That is the story, the story of grace.

As Moses says, *[You] cannot afford the offerings that would be required for our [your] cleansing* **[Leviticus 14:32]**.

This is why the Bible says,

And many lepers were in Israel in the time of Eliseus the prophet; and none of them was cleansed, saving Naaman the Syrian **[Luke 4:27]**.

This was Jesus speaking. Jesus did not read about the story of Naaman, Jesus was in the healing of Naaman.

Leprosy is more than skin deep; it is filthiness of the skin and spirit.

Paul says,

Having therefore these promises, dearly beloved, let us cleanse ourselves from all filthiness of the flesh and spirit, perfecting holiness in the fear of God **[2 Corinthians 7:1]**.

David says, *purge me with hyssop, and I shall be clean: wash me, and I shall be whiter than snow* **[Psalm 51:7]**.

Our God does not change. We can and we will get healed.

Blindness

Being blind is hard.

Blind Bartimaeus cried a lot when he heard Jesus was passing by.

How could he let such an opportunity pass?

*And they came to Jericho: and as he went out of Jericho with his disciples and a great number of people, blind Bartimaeus, the son of Timaeus, sat by the highway side begging **[Mark 10:46]**.*

This is Jericho, the city of the palm trees.

Yet someone is crying because he is blind.

Jesus walked intentionally close by, because He knew, blind Bartimaeus was sitting right there.

The blind man decided he had begged enough, he could not continue to beg when Jesus was passing by.

It did not matter what the others thought. He was going to be healed, not the following day.

How could he let an opportunity pass, an opportunity to see.

Blind Bartimaeus knew opportunity and chance comes to all men.

Bartimaeus was going to take his chance with Jesus.

The blind man was going to tell his story, I "saw" an opportunity pass, and I would not let it go.

Begging has never been good, it makes you feel small.

You do not beg because you are blind, you beg because you cannot see.

Physical blindness is sense impairment, not being able to see is a mind and heart impairment.

With eyes open, most fail to see the grace of God; fail to see opportunity to tell their story.

They are too conscious of the crowd. They have no vision for the Godly.

^{47} And when he heard that it was Jesus of Nazareth, he began to cry out, and say, Jesus, thou son of David, have mercy on me. ^{48} And many charged him that he should hold his peace: but he cried the more a great deal, Thou son of David, have mercy on me [Mark 10:47-48].

Jesus did not ask that the blind man be brought to him.

He commanded that he be called.

A person that has been called walks on their own.

The path is clear to them. They know who called and from where.

Jesus stood still, because "blind" Bartimaeus could see Jesus.

*⁴⁹ And Jesus stood still, and commanded him to be called. And they call the blind man, saying unto him, Be of good comfort, rise; he calleth thee. ⁵⁰ And he, casting away his garment, rose, and came to Jesus. ⁵¹ And Jesus answered and said unto him, What wilt thou that I should do unto thee? The blind man said unto him, Lord, that I might receive my sight. ⁵² And Jesus said unto him, Go thy way; thy faith hath made thee whole. And immediately he received his sight, and followed Jesus in the way **[Mark 10:49-52]**.*

The "blind" cast off his garment, Jesus is seeing the blind. Not in their physical but in their spiritual.

The world gives statistics on the physically blind.

In the spiritual, the physically blind may actually see better than the spiritually blind, the mentally blind and the socially blind.

In the crowd that followed Jesus were more blind people than anyone cared to count.

A grace story is told by the faithful. The faith in Bartimaeus shouted, the faith in Bartimaeus cast off the begging garment, the plate and all.

The faith in Bartimaeus cried out for attention, the faith in Bartimaeus saw the opportunity.

Jesus was right there. Jesus had made His way to the blind. Everyone who wants to see has to call.

Blindness is not just of the eyes. Its blindness to what is right, what is good, what is true.

Bartimaeus had to shout, to cry so his voice could rise above the noise of the crowd.

The noise of the crowd is huge; the noise of doubt, of sin, of unforgiveness, of disobedience.

Blind people know they are blind, only they can choose to call or to keep quiet.

Leprosy is gone, blindness is gone. The balm of Gilead passed my way. He is the great physician.

Redeemed, redeemed, redeemed, is my story too.

> Redeemed, how I love to proclaim it!
> Redeemed by the blood of the Lamb;
> Redeemed through His infinite mercy,
> His child and forever I am.

> *Refrain:*
> Redeemed, redeemed,

Redeemed by the blood of the Lamb;
Redeemed, redeemed,
His child and forever I am.

Redeemed, and so happy in Jesus,
No language my rapture can tell;
I know that the light of His presence
With me doth continually dwell.

I think of my blessed Redeemer,
I think of Him all the day long:
I sing, for I cannot be silent;
His love is the theme of my song.

I know I shall see in His beauty
The King in whose law I delight;
Who lovingly guardeth my footsteps,
And giveth me songs in the night.

I know there's a crown that is waiting
In yonder bright mansion for me,
And soon, with the spirits made perfect,
At home with the Lord I shall be.

J. Crosby 1882 Timeless Truths Free Online Library

Lord, I love the habitation of your house and the place where your glory dwells [Psalms 26:8].

CHAPTER 9

THE MAGNIFICENT GOD

The Creator

There are things that happen in our lives that make us so happy, so joyful, and so content.

It is like the rain falling after a long drought. Often, however, the rains that fall to cut the drought come with thunderstorms, lightings, floods and mudslides.

When that happens, that would not be what we expected.

We would have just expected a good crop and a good harvest.

The question then is; why the floods, the mudslides, the thunderstorms and the lightning?

Why?

My understanding of God is; the magnificence of God cannot be seen in quiet waters, it is best seen in the rapids and the waterfalls.

God is seen in the recovery and restoration from a debilitating disease.

God is seen, not in the drizzling rain, but in the thunder and the lightning.

God is seen in our faith.

To Job God says He is in the clouds, in the size of the leviathan, in the fearless ness and strength of the horse and in the "misunderstood stupidity" of the ostrich.

To His disciples, Jesus says,

*^{6} .... I am the way, the truth, and the life: no man cometh unto the Father, but by me.^{7} If ye had known me, ye should have known my Father also: and from henceforth ye know him, and have seen him.^{8} Philip saith unto him, Lord, show us the Father, and it sufficeth us. ^{9} Jesus saith unto him, Have I been so long time with you, and yet hast thou not known me, Philip? he that hath seen me hath seen the Father; and how sayest thou then, Show us the Father?^{10} Believest thou not that I am in the Father, and the Father in me? the words that I speak unto you I speak not of myself: but the Father that dwelleth in me, he doeth the works **[John 14:6-10].***

God in our challenges

The Bible says,

*There was a man in the land of Uz, whose name was Job; and that man was perfect and upright, and one that feared God, and eschewed evil **[Job 1-21].***

God knew this man, where he lived, what he did and what he had.

Job new that *the fear of the LORD is the beginning of wisdom: and the knowledge of the holy is understanding **[Proverbs 9:10]**.*

Job knew *the steps of a good man are ordered by the LORD: and he delighteth in his way **[Psalms 37:23]**.*

Job knew that only God perfects, *¹⁴ For by one offering he hath perfected for ever them that are sanctified **[Hebrews 10:14]**.*

Job was the man the Bible says *was the greatest of all the men of the east **[Job 1:3]**.*

Perfect and upright as Job was, fearing God, and avoiding all evil, in his walk and in his conversations, the rains, the thunderstorms and the lightning, came.

Job was meticulous in how he handled the things of God.

Job knew God as God, the Creator of the Universe, the Giver of Life.

Job would give a sacrifice for forgiveness, *for Job said, It may be that my sons have sinned, and cursed God in their hearts. Thus did Job continually **[Job 1:5]**.*

When the rains came, all was lost. He was left a pauper, he was left without health.

He moved from being great, to the least in his society.

It was difficult, it was hard, it was challenging.

God does not make an excuse to Job, God does not apologise to Job, and God did not explain anything to Job.

God asks Job some questions, from *Job 37 to 39*.

At the end Job says *I have heard of thee by the hearing of the ear: but now mine eye seeth thee [Job 42:5].*

Job understood, as the Psalmist said,

As for God, his way is perfect: the word of the LORD is tried: he is a buckler to all those that trust in him [Psalms 18:30].

God asks Job, do you *know the balancings of the clouds, the wondrous works of him which is perfect in knowledge? [Job 37:16].*

Canst thou lift up thy voice to the clouds, that abundance of waters may cover thee? ^{35} Canst thou send lightnings, that they may go and say unto thee, Here we are [Job 38:34-35].

Gavest thou the wings and feathers unto the ostrich? ^{14} Which leaveth her eggs in the earth, and warmeth them in dust, ^{15} And forgetteth that the foot may crush them, or that the wild beast may break them^{17} Because God hath deprived her of wisdom, neither hath he imparted to her understanding. YET ^{18} *What time she lifteth up herself on high, she scorneth the horse and his rider. [Job 39:13-25].*

Wow!

To Job, this was most assuring.

To me, this is the magnificence of our God.

The Lord gave the ostrich what man says is foolishness, yet the same God says when the ostrich decides to challenge her situation, the horse and its rider have no chance!

As I read the book of Job, I was fascinated by the way our God interacted with Job.

I decided to check this out, the ostrich and the horse.

I was simply excited as I read the following:

An article on ostriches indicated that when the ostrich runs, the other animals know they should run too.

An ostrich can run faster than most horses.

It was an interesting fact that lions live where ostriches do.

Ostriches have strength to match any forest, any plain, any valley and any hill.

Ostriches live where lions do!

It was recorded that an ostrich's powerful, long legs can cover 10 to 16 feet in a single stride.

These legs can also be formidable weapons. Ostrich kicks can kill a human or a potential predator, even a lion.

The kicks are powerful, such that an Ostrich can kick with a force of about 2,000 pounds per square inch, which is 141 kg per square cm.

Google.com. *Speed of ostrich at full flight*
[Accessed 04/12/2018].

Masai Ostrich

Wikipedia.org. [September 1, 2009]Male Ostrich in Ngorongoro.
[Accessed December 2018]

In comparison, galloping, the horse can do 40-48 kilometres an hour, although for short sprints, the fastest galloping speed is achieved by the American Quarter Horse, which in a short sprint of a quarter mile [0.25 miles [0.40 km] or less, has been clocked at speeds approaching 55 miles per hour [88.5 km/h].

Wikipedia.org.https://en.wikipedia.org/wiki/
Fastest_animals [Accessed December 4, 2018]

It is also recorded that a horse's kick can exert anywhere from zero to more than 2,000 pounds of pressure per square inch.

Lemen.com. [2006] Questions and Answers
[Accessed December 4, 2018]

God the Creator asks Job,

19 Hast thou given the horse strength? hast thou clothed his neck with thunder? 20 Canst thou make him afraid as a grasshopper? the glory of his nostrils is terrible. 21 He paweth in the valley, and rejoiceth in his strength: he goeth on to meet the armed men. 22 He mocketh at fear, and is not affrighted; neither turneth he back from the sword. 23 The quiver rattleth against him, the glittering spear and the shield. 24 He swalloweth the ground with fierceness and rage.... 25.... and he smelleth the battle afar off, the thunder of the captains, and the shouting [Job 39:19-25].

Job had probably not done the maths on ostriches and horses.

At the end of Job's struggles, Job new who God was.

Job understood God, as much as Paul did when Paul said to the Romans,

*^{33} O the depth of the riches both of the wisdom and knowledge of God! how unsearchable are his judgments, and his ways past finding out!^{34} For who hath known the mind of the Lord? or who hath been his counsellor?^{35} Or who hath first given to him, and it shall be recompensed unto him again?^{36} For of him, and through him, and to him, are all things: to whom be glory for ever. Amen **[Romans 11:33-36].***

The Creator gave the facts. He was there; He is there, in everything.

This is the magnificence of God.

When life is challenging, I have learnt this fact, that God's ways are not our ways.

I have learnt that Jesus is the way, the truth and the life.

I have learnt to trust the Creator of the Universe, even when everything else tells me otherwise.

I have learnt that even me, I can stand tall as the Masai Ostrich, against the lions of the Masai Mara.

I have learnt, I can stand, with my head lifted up, as the Appaloosa horse, because the Lord God is the lifter of my head, just as David did, in the songs of all seasons.

David says, *³But thou, O Lord, art a shield for me; my glory, and the lifter up of mine head **[Psalms 3:3]**.*

Appaloosa Horse
wikipedia.org/wiki/Appaloosa
[Accessed December 4, 2018]

God is magnificent; it is grace to know the Lord. David could then say,

*One thing have I desired of the LORD, that will I seek after; that I may dwell in the house of the LORD all the days of my life, to behold the beauty of the LORD, and to enquire in his temple **[Psalm 27:4]**.*

This is the Lord who says to the rains, to the thunderstorms and the lightning in our lives,

*Hitherto shalt thou come, but no further: and here shall thy proud waves be stayed **[Job 38:11]**.*

Our God, is the most merciful father!

When life comes, with incessant rains and mudslides, our father is there, to see us through, for He is the Lord God Almighty.

When God is there, there are always survivors!

The adage goes, hope is a weapon, and survival is victory.

Victory comes from the Lord.

During incessant rains, we call heaven, and God hears.

The Lord is attentive – thus far and no further, and the rains stop.

Some will perish with the floods and the mudslides, but others will survive.

There is a reason why survivors survive. Survivors prepare to survive when it rains incessantly.

The everyday supplies, the accessible rain proof shelters, the clothes, the communication equipment, the light, the ropes, everything. These make the difference.

Rains are found anywhere on the planet.

Even in the dry desert, rains periodically fall.

Rains come in different months or seasons; some in January some in May, some in August and anytime in between.

These differ by location, in intensity and in magnitude, but by definition, they are all rains.

It is grace that rainy seasons come and go. They do not stay forever. The floods and the mudslides give us more revelation, on the magnificence of God.

We can then say like Paul;

*For I am persuaded, that neither death, nor life, nor angels, nor principalities, nor powers, nor things present, nor things to come, ^{39} Nor height, nor depth, nor any other creature, shall be able to separate us from the love of God, which is in Christ Jesus our Lord **[Romans 8:38-39]**.*

It is grace that gives peace, even in the midst of a rainy season.

Built on God we will say,

*And the peace of God, which passeth all understanding, shall keep your hearts and minds through Christ Jesus **[Philippians 4:7]**.*

We will also sing, every day,

> O God, our help in ages past,
> Our hope for years to come,
> Our shelter from the stormy blast,
> And our eternal home.
>
> Under the shadow of Thy throne
> Thy saints have dwelt secure;
> Sufficient is Thine arm alone,
> And our defence is sure.
>
> Before the hills in order stood,
> Or earth received her frame,
> From everlasting Thou art God,
> To endless years the same.
>
> Thy Word commands our flesh to dust,
> "Return, ye sons of men":
> All nations rose from earth at first,
> And turn to earth again.

A thousand ages in Thy sight
Are like an evening gone;
Short as the watch that ends the night
Before the rising sun.

The busy tribes of flesh and blood,
With all their lives and cares,
Are carried downwards by the flood,
And lost in foll'wing years.

Time, like an ever-rolling stream,
Bears all its sons away;
They fly, forgotten, as a dream
Dies at the op'ning day.

Like flow'ry fields the nations stand
Pleased with the morning light;
The flow'rs beneath the mower's hand
Lie with'ring ere 'tis night.

O God, our help in ages past,
Our hope for years to come,
Be Thou our guard while troubles last,
And our eternal home.

Isaac Watts 1719 Timeless Truths Free Online Library.

Grateful For Grace

Tribute To My God

I cannot end the writing of this chapter, without writing my praise, even though I do not have words enough, in shape or form, to pay homage, to honour or to worship my God.

What I know is:

My God cares, even for the little details of my life,

My God covers me, all day long, sleeping or waking,

My God loves me,

My God knows my name……..,

My God is a magnificent God, to me and to you also!

O God, our help in ages past, Our hope for years to come, Be Thou our guard while troubles last, And our eternal home **[Isaac Watts]**.

Lord, I love the habitation of your house and the place where your glory dwells [Psalms 26:8].

CHAPTER 10

THE DESERT FOUNTAIN

Living Water

Barrenness, emptiness and a sense of desolation, is typical of deserts.

There is no promise of life. Deserts create a sense of hopelessness.

In a desert, unless created for the desert, survival is a challenge.

There is always a feeling of foreboding, fearful apprehension, and uncertainty, all because there is no water or there is very little water.

For life, water is everything.

Jesus quickly assures,

14... whosoever drinketh of the water that I shall give him shall never thirst; but the water that I shall give him shall be in him a well of water springing up into everlasting life [John 4:14].

Jesus goes on, *[38] He that believeth on me, as the scripture hath said, out of his belly shall flow rivers of living water [John 7:38].*

Needless to say, the world we live is a great desert, a wilderness.

There are poisonous scorpions, there are sharp stones, there are dust storms, and there is heat, day and night, in the desert.

Temperatures can be extreme, whether day or night.

When it is hot, it is extreme, when it is cold, it is also extreme.

Whilst the extremities differ, from desert to desert, from person to person, the impact is the same.

Life is a huge challenge, in desert territory. There is a lot of anxiety and a lot of crying.

But to the children of Israel, Moses says,

For the LORD thy God hath blessed thee in all the works of thy hand: he knoweth thy walking through this great wilderness: these forty years the LORD thy God hath been with thee; thou hast lacked nothing. ***[Deuteronomy 2:7].***

The Almighty God is the fountain that gives life in the desert.

The extreme temperatures will still be there, and so will be the scorpions and the sharp stones, but all would not matter, because there is water.

The grace of God cannot be explained, even for the desert.

It has been studied that, generally, desert fountains do not ordinarily dry up, because they are meant to sustain life in the desert.

Desert fountains can have bitter water, but not dry.

That place of bitter waters, with God, is the place of grace.

By the grace of God, the water will be made sweet, the garments will be washed, the stock will be fed and drink, there will be laughter, everyone is refreshed.

Desert life is distressful. It does not matter where you live or who you are.

The Lord God says to Isaiah,

*[18] I will open rivers in high places, and fountains in the midst of the valleys: I will make the wilderness a pool of water, and the dry land springs of water. [19] I will plant in the wilderness the cedar, the shittah tree, and the myrtle, and the oil tree; I will set in the desert the fir tree, and the pine, and the box tree together: [20] That they may see, and know, and consider, and understand together, that the hand of the LORD hath done this, and the Holy One of Israel hath created it **[Isaiah 41:18-20]***

With God, nothing becomes "typical" of deserts.

Desert

Google.com. Typical Desert.https://www.google.com/
[Accessed October 12, 2018]

As the Bible says, the Lord said to Moses, concerning the children of Israel;

I have surely seen the affliction of my people which are in Egypt, and have heard their cry by reason of their taskmasters; for I know their sorrows; 8 And I am come down to deliver them 9 Now therefore, behold, the cry of the children of Israel is come unto me: and I have also seen the oppression wherewith the Egyptians oppress them **[Exodus 3:7-10]**.

The children of Israel had a hard life in Egypt, a life of slavery.

Slavery comes in many ways and forms.

What defines slavery is the level of distress!

David says,

*In my distress I called upon the LORD, and cried unto my God: he heard my voice out of his temple, and my cry came before him, even into his ears **[Psalms 18:6].***

David had so many challenges, from Saul the king to Absalom his son.

He was a king of Israel but that did not save him from the tears.

David had the hill advantage, he knew how to cry.

Nobody else had to hear, as your cry may be someone's joke.

All others will take away whatever of you was left. Only God hears the way we want to be heard.

That is grace.

Being heard is awesome, just being heard.

Under the mudslides, in the floods, in the thunderstorms of this life, it is by God's grace that we are heard when we cry in our distress.

What distresses is a lot, from sin to disease to any form of disability.

The Lord comes down in fire and glory, to change situations and circumstances.

The Bible says,

*³ And when all the children of Israel saw how the fire came down, and the glory of the LORD upon the house, they bowed themselves with their faces to the ground upon the pavement, and worshipped, and praised the LORD, saying, For he is good; for his mercy endureth for ever **[2 chronicles 7:3]**.*

Sin distresses as much as poverty, disease and fear, but the Lord's mercies endure - for ever.

Sodom and Gomorrah cried because of sin, Sodom and Gomorrah were cities distressed by sin.

The Bible says,

*²⁰ And the LORD said, Because the cry of Sodom and Gomorrah is great, and because their sin is very grievous; ²¹ I will go down now, and see whether they have done altogether according to the cry of it, which is come unto me; and if not, I will know. ²² And the men turned their faces from thence, and went toward Sodom: but Abraham stood yet before the LORD **[Genesis 18:20-22]**.*

There is no survival unless and until we see the fountain.

Hagar saw the fountain, and lived.

In Genesis chapter 16, things got bad for Hagar, and she ran,

Wrong or right, Hagar had to run.

She had conceived where the other could not. She was proud, because she could.

What then happened happened, and she had to run.

*⁷ And the angel of the LORD found her by a fountain of water in the wilderness, by the fountain in the way to Shur. ¹⁰ And the angel of the LORD said unto her, I will multiply thy seed exceedingly, that it shall not be numbered for multitude. ¹¹ And the angel of the LORD said unto her, Behold, thou art with child and shalt bear a son, and shalt call his name Ishmael; because the LORD hath heard thy affliction **[Genesis 16:7-11]**.*

Hagar did not give her son a name. God gave Ishmael his name.

The runaway servant is relating with God.

The run-away servant gets a promise from God.

The promise is made in the desert.

Even Sarah could not have imagined.

That was grace.

The Lord says of Ishmael,

*And as for Ishmael, I have heard thee: Behold, I have blessed him, and will make him fruitful, and will multiply him exceedingly; twelve princes shall he beget, and I will make him a great nation **[Genesis 17:20]**.*

This is grace.

Sarah got twelve tribes through Jacob, so did Hagar – twelve princes God promised.

God is fair. It is all grace.

Laughter

After crossing the desert, there is relief, there is laughter.

There was laughter when the children of Israel crossed the Jordan. Not for a few, but for everyone.

For fourty years they lacked nothing, yet they could not rejoice, they could not laugh. They were not home, regardless of God's provisions in the desert.

They needed to get home.

Once, they were in Canaan, and they left for Egypt because of famine.

Centuries later, it took them fourty years to cross over a week's journey distance.

As God would have it, God led the children of Israel through desert country so that they would appreciate Canaan.

The Bible says,

*^{10} But when ye go over Jordan, and dwell in the land which the LORD your God giveth you to inherit, and when he giveth you rest from all your enemies round about, so that ye dwell in safety;…… ^{12} And ye shall rejoice before the LORD your God, ye, and your sons, and your daughters, and your menservants, and your maidservants, and the Levite that is within your gates **[Deuteronomy 12]**.*

When you get home you know its home.

You eat the old corn, because the manna was for the desert.

When the manna ceased, they were home.

God's grace provides, all things for all seasons.

The Bible says,

*^{12} And the manna ceased on the morrow after they had eaten of the old corn of the land; neither had the children of Israel manna anymore; but they did eat of the fruit of the land of Canaan that year **[Joshua 5:12]**.*

It does not matter what we go through, God's grace is sufficient.

We will tell our story, the fourty year journey, to our children and our children's children.

We cannot waver; we cannot doubt the provisions of the Lord.

God will defend our laughter.

His sword is drawn up, just like He did across the Jordan.

When Joshua was by Jericho, *he lifted up his eyes and looked, and, behold, there stood a man over against him with his sword drawn in his hand: and Joshua went unto him, and said unto him, Art thou for us, or for our adversaries? ¹⁴ And he said, Nay; but as captain of the host of the LORD am I now come. And Joshua fell on his face to the earth, and did worship [Joshua 5:13-14].*

This is our God, the defender of our faith.

God stood ready to defend the children of Israel across the Jordan.

God so defended our faith when Jesus was raised on Calvary's mountain.

Here or there, our road to Canaan is secured, and our laughter was guaranteed.

There was grace in the building of the cross. That cross was balance.

As much as God is in all our seasons and in all our places, God was in the darkness and the earthquake on Calvary too.

And as Moses lifted up the serpent in the wilderness, even so must the Son of man be lifted up: ⁵That whosoever believeth in him should not perish, but have eternal life [John 3:14-15].

The cross was God's way. God was not playing dice – not with man, not with His son.

It was God's way to our salvation.

Now we sing;

> Jesus, keep me near the cross,
> There a precious fountain—
> Free to all, a healing stream—
> Flows from Calv'ry's mountain.
>
> Refrain:
> In the cross, in the cross,
> Be my glory ever;
> Till my raptured soul shall find
> Rest beyond the river.
>
> Near the cross, a trembling soul,

Love and Mercy found me;
There the bright and morning star
Sheds its beams around me.

Near the cross! O Lamb of God,
Bring its scenes before me;
Help me walk from day to day,
With its shadows o'er me.

Near the cross I'll watch and wait
Hoping, trusting ever,
Till I reach the golden strand,
Just beyond the river.

[Fanny J. Crosby and Wm H. Doane] 1869
Timeless Truths Free Online Library

The fountain that was in the desert for Hagar was also on Calvary.

The cross that was raised in the desert by Moses was also on Calvary.

Promises were made to Hagar and so too to the children of Israel.

To Hagar it was abundance.

To the children of Israel it was laughter,

Both were after the desert, and the cross was built for us.

We are fitly framed together, so that we can cross the desert.

As Paul says,

*In whom [Christ] all the building fitly framed together groweth unto an holy temple in the Lord: ^{22} In whom ye also are builded together for an habitation of God through the Spirit **[Ephesians 2:21-22]**.*

Fitly framed together, the scorpions will not matter, nor the sharp stones, as we leave behind the distress of desert life.

Everything, everything, works together so that we can get to the cross, the messiest of all building sites, yet most magnificently full of mercy.

> ***Lord, I love the habitation of your house and the place where your glory dwells [Psalms 26:8].***

CHAPTER 11

BUILDING FOR GOD

300 Cubits Long

God gave man a lot of freedoms.

Of the many freedoms given to man, I consider these two; to build, and to name.

In Genesis, God asked Adam to name the animals and Adam named the animals in the manner God had expected *[Genesis 2:19-20]*.

God gave instructions to build to Noah and the building was built as per instructions *[Genesis 6:13-22]*.

To Moses He did too and the ark was a replica of the one in heaven *[Exodus 25]*.

But at Babel it was a different story.

The instructions at Babel did not come from heaven.

When the all-seeing God saw what man was doing at Babel and read man's heart, God said, let us go down and see.

Really?

God did not need to go down; He did not need a special mission to see.

God needed no evidence.

God knew and He knows the end from the beginning.

The people at the tower were like a much loved child.

Parents watch, actually go and see them perform when the parent taught the child the script.

The parents applaud when really they already knew what the child could and could not do.

Parents are fascinated by their children, young or old.

Could we say God was fascinated by man?

It is possible. The Bible says God said let us go down.

This means building is significant. Whatever we build, says a lot about our heart.

Before Babel, there was Noah.

The Bible says,

Noah was a just man and perfect in his generations, and Noah walked with God. And God said unto Noah, The end of all flesh is come before me; for the earth is filled with violence through them; and, behold, I will destroy them with the earth. [14] Make thee an ark of gopher wood; rooms shalt thou make in the ark, and shalt pitch it within and without with pitch. [15] And this is the fashion which thou shalt make it of: The length of the ark shall be three hundred cubits, the breadth of it fifty cubits, and the height of it thirty cubits. [16] A window shalt thou make to the ark, and in a cubit shalt thou finish it above; and the door of the ark shalt thou set in the side thereof; with lower, second, and third stories shalt thou make it [Genesis 6:9-16].

Noah listened, Noah did exactly as the Lord had indicated, because Noah knew, God was and is the master builder.

God built three stories up!

Wow.

Building for God starts with God.

God has a floor for the threesome power of heaven!

And all God does is premised on saving. Saving the man He created.

When Noah built, the project was for all flesh - everything made of dust; man, animal, bird, the creeping and the crawling.

God says,

[17] And, behold, I, even I, do bring a flood of waters upon the earth, to destroy all flesh, wherein is the breath of life, from under heaven; and everything that

is in the earth shall die. ^{18} But with thee will I establish my covenant; and thou shalt come into the ark, thou, and thy sons, and thy wife, and thy sons' wives with thee [Genesis 6:17-18].

This is the evidence of Amos the prophet.

The Bible says,

Surely the Lord GOD will do nothing, but he revealeth his secret unto his servants the prophets [Amos 3:7].

The Bibles goes further,

^{19} And of every living thing of all flesh, two of every sort shalt thou bring into the ark, to keep them alive with thee; they shall be male and female. ^{20} Of fowls after their kind, and of cattle after their kind, of every creeping thing of the earth after his kind, two of every sort shall come unto thee, to keep them alive [Genesis 6:19-20].

Noah built for God – to keep alive what God had created.

Just and perfect, walking with God, Noah could not be lost.

Noah had to live, together with everything else God created.

This was grace.

[21] And take thou unto thee of all food that is eaten, and thou shalt gather it to thee; and it shall be for food for thee, and for them. [22] Thus did Noah; according to all that God commanded him, so did he **[Genesis 6:21-22]**.

Noah ended up on Mt Ararat, and we have the evidence.

This was God's doing.

This is a story of grace.

Noah's efforts were not in vain, as the Bible says,

And God blessed Noah and his sons, and said unto them, Be fruitful, and multiply, and replenish the earth. [2] And the fear of you and the dread of you shall be upon every beast of the earth, and upon every fowl of the air, upon all that moveth upon the earth, and upon all the fishes of the sea; into your hand are they delivered... [9] And I, behold, I establish my covenant with you, and with your seed after you; [10] And with every living creature that is with you, [15] And I will remember my covenant, which is between me and you and every living creature of all flesh; and the waters shall no more become a flood to destroy all flesh [8] And Noah lived after the flood three hundred and fifty years. [29] And all the days of Noah were nine hundred and fifty years: and he died **[Genesis 9:1-2]**.

Noah's Ark
Pininterest.com. The Ark on Mount Ararat
[Accessed January 29, 2019].

God acknowledged Noah and gave him years to his life.

The Bible says,

And it came to pass, when men began to multiply on the face of the earth.....³ And the LORD said, My spirit shall not always strive with man, for that he also is flesh: yet his days shall be an hundred and twenty years……..⁷ And the LORD said, I will destroy man whom I have created from the face of the earth; both man, and beast, and the creeping thing, and the fowls of the air; for it repenteth me that I have made them........ ⁸But Noah found grace in the eyes of the LORD [Genesis 6:1-8].

The Lord had said man's days shall be 120, but Noah lived to 900 years.

What a blessing.

Noah built to specifications.

God's instructions are not vague, neither are they burdensome.

God knew exactly 300 cubits would carry all types of creatures, great and small.

God knew the weight of the sevens and the twos.

God knew the weight of the food they would eat.

The Bible does not tell how Noah got the water, yet Bible scholars indicate Noah was in the ark for between three hundred and sixty four [364] and three hundred and seventy [370] days.

Awesome grace.

And A Half

The children of Israel also built, and Moses was the Building Inspector!

The Lord says,

⁸ And let them make me a sanctuary; that I may dwell among them. ⁹ According to all that I shew thee, after the pattern of the tabernacle, and the pattern of all the instruments thereof, even so shall ye make it.¹⁰... two cubits and a half shall be the length thereof, and a cubit and a half the breadth thereof, and a cubit and a half the height thereof.......¹⁶ And thou shalt put into the ark the testimony which I shall give thee **[Exodus 25:8-16]**.

The Mercy Seat

¹⁷ And thou shalt make a mercy seat of pure gold: two cubits and a half shall be the length thereof, and a cubit and a half the breadth thereof.... ²¹ And thou shalt put the mercy seat above upon the ark; and in the ark thou shalt put the testimony that I shall give thee. ²² And there I will meet with thee, and I will commune with thee from above the mercy seat **[Exodus 25:17-22]**.

As God was leading a very mixed multitude of people out of Egypt, people who would test God's love and patience, the mercy seat gave life to an otherwise "unworthy" congregation.

The Lord wanted two cubits and a half for the length, and a cubit and a half the width.

God wanted those halves. Moses just listened.

The Bible says,

⁴² According to all that the LORD commanded Moses, so the children of Israel made all the work. ⁴³ And Moses did look upon all the work, and, behold, they had done it as the LORD had commanded, even so had they done it: and Moses blessed them [Exodus 39].

All Moses built was for testimony; it was evidence of awesome power, awesome grace.

Someone had to tell that story.

Caleb and Joshua did.

In my view, Noah built the most magnificent ship of all ages – Noah's ark.

Moses oversaw the building of the most magnificent symbol of all time - the Ark of the Covenant.

Then a man built the Tomb....

Joseph of Arimathea

I have always been fascinated by Joseph of Arimathea.

His involvement with Jesus the Christ does not take up much space in the Bible.

I am amazed by what he did.

The Bible says he was a disciple of Christ, a member of the Sanhedrin but who would not vote to send Christ to the cross.

God's plans for our lives are unsearchable, they are grand.

Joseph of Arimathea was woven into the intricacies of our salvation centuries before Joseph of Arimathea was born.

For Isaiah says of Jesus,

*And he made his grave with the wicked, and with the rich in his death; because he had done no violence, neither was any deceit in his mouth **[Isaiah 53:9]**.*

Arguably, Isaiah is foretelling the story of Jesus and Joseph of Arimathea.

This Joseph built a tomb, a grave, for God, as no other man was ever buried in that grave, even Joseph of Arimathea.

Joseph of Arimathea had probably never read the book of Isaiah.

Mathew wrote four [4] verses about Joseph of Arimathea.

Mathew says,

When the even was come, there came a rich man of Arimathaea, named Joseph, who also himself was Jesus' disciple: [58] He went to Pilate, and begged the body of Jesus. Then Pilate commanded the body to be delivered. [59] And when Joseph had taken the body, he wrapped it in a clean linen cloth, [60] And laid it in his own new tomb, which he had hewn out in the rock: and he rolled a great stone to the door of the sepulchre, and departed [Mathew 27:57-60].

When Joseph hewed the rock to create his tomb, he probably never imagined he was not going to be buried in that grave.

The Bible does not tell us how many people "dug" their graves on rocks, but Joseph did.

The whole process had to fit the scriptures.

Three days Jesus had to be in the tomb.

It would have taken much longer to start and finish "digging" *out in the rock* after Jesus had died.

The time would not have added up.

Jesus was and is, the rock of all ages.

How could dust have contained Him?

The Bible says, *and he rolled a great stone to the door of the sepulchre, and departed;*

This is amazing. It took the angel of God to remove the stone when Jesus rose.

To me, Joseph and Nicodemus could not have rolled the stone to close the tomb, after they had buried Jesus.

John says they were two, and the ladies were witnesses.

I keep asking - how did Joseph and Nicodemus close the tomb – who rolled the stone to close the tomb?

As the Bible says, it was a great stone.

My thinking is, Joseph was just the "hand that wrote on the wall", in the story of Belteshazzar.

The Lord God, the Father, closed the tomb where His son had just been buried.

The assigned angels rolled the stone to the grave; the angels were going to also roll it away on the third day.

Mark adds a fifth verse to this amazing story.

As Mark tells his story, Mary Magdalene and Mary the Mother of Jesus were there, with Joseph of Arimathea.

The resources, the heart, the body and the mind went into the burial of Jesus.

And the angels of heaven were also there, not just as witnesses, but actively involved.

Mark says, *Joseph of Arimathaea, an honourable counsellor, which also waited for the kingdom of God, came, and went in boldly unto Pilate, and craved the body of Jesus. [44] And Pilate marvelled if he were already dead: and calling unto him the centurion, he asked him whether he had been any while dead. [45] And when he knew it of the centurion, he gave the body to Joseph. [46] And he bought fine linen, and took him down, and wrapped him in the linen, and laid him in a sepulchre which was hewn out of a rock, and rolled a stone unto the door of the sepulchre. [47] And Mary Magdalene and Mary the mother of Jesus beheld where he was laid [Mark 15:43-47].*

Pilate marvelled. The cross was heaven on show.

The hour had been set thousands of years earlier, the space was perfect, outside the camp, so that the man with leprosy could and can also see and find Jesus.

It had to be on top of the hill, the best defensive position in any warfare.

If Joseph had not gone to ask for the body of Jesus, Pilate would not have known that indeed Jesus was the son of God.

Luke adds a little more detail.

Luke says the Sabbath was near. This was a well "rehearsed script".

Everything had to be right, and on time.

God was in everything, for the Bible says,

He [God] set His throne in the heavens, and beholds everything done on the earth [Psalms 103:19].

Luke says,

And, behold, there was a man named Joseph, a counsellor; and he was a good man, and a just: ^{51} [The same had not consented to the counsel and deed of them;]. he was of Arimathaea, a city of the Jews: who also himself waited for the kingdom of God. ^{52} This man went unto Pilate, and begged the body of Jesus. ^{53} And he took it down, and wrapped it in linen, and laid it in a sepulchre that was hewn in stone, wherein never man before was laid. ^{54} And that day was the preparation, and the sabbath drew on.^{55} And the women also, which came with him from Galilee, followed after, and beheld the sepulchre, *and how his body was laid [Luke 23:50-56].*

In Joseph of Arimathea, God had built up a man who would be around on the day, in time, in place and in space.

That man had to be good and just, even Pilate would not doubt his intensions.

How would Pilate give the body of Christ to a man?

This man Joseph was asking for was as powerful in death as when alive.

The Bible records Jesus would be seen in specific places, He had risen from the dead!

How could Pilate have agreed, unless God the Father was also in the darkness and the earthquake on Calvary?

John adds a little more.

John says,

And after this Joseph of Arimathaea, being a disciple of Jesus, but secretly for fear of the Jews, besought Pilate that he might take away the body of Jesus: and Pilate gave him leave. He came therefore, and took the body of Jesus. ^{39} And there came also Nicodemus, which at the first came to Jesus by night, and brought a mixture of myrrh and aloes, about an hundred pound weight. ^{40} Then took they the body of Jesus, and wound it in linen clothes with the spices, as the manner of the Jews is to bury. ^{41} Now in the place where he was crucified there was a garden; and in the garden a new sepulchre, wherein was never man yet laid. ^{42} There laid they Jesus therefore because of the Jews' preparation day; for the sepulchre was nigh at hand **[John 19:38-42].**

Joseph was of Arimathea, a city of the Jews.

He was counted with them yet not one of them.

Joseph was taller, reinforced by heaven for this day.

Joseph of Arimathea was built for purpose.

Jesus had to be buried. Joseph of Arimathea's grave was near. God had instructed it be built there.

Joseph had, inadvertently, been building for God.

Joseph of Arimathea's home was in Arimathea, miles away from Jerusalem.

Logic would say Joseph would have been buried in Arimathea, but he "chose" to prepare his grave just close to Calvary, in time for Jesus burial.

What coincidence!

No, it was not coincidence, for there is no coincidence in the things of God. It is all very intentional.

Joseph of Arimathea could have said, like Solomon,

But will God in very deed dwell [be buried] with men on the earth? behold, heaven and the heaven of heavens cannot contain thee; how much less this house [grave] which I have built! ***[2 Chronicles 6:18].***

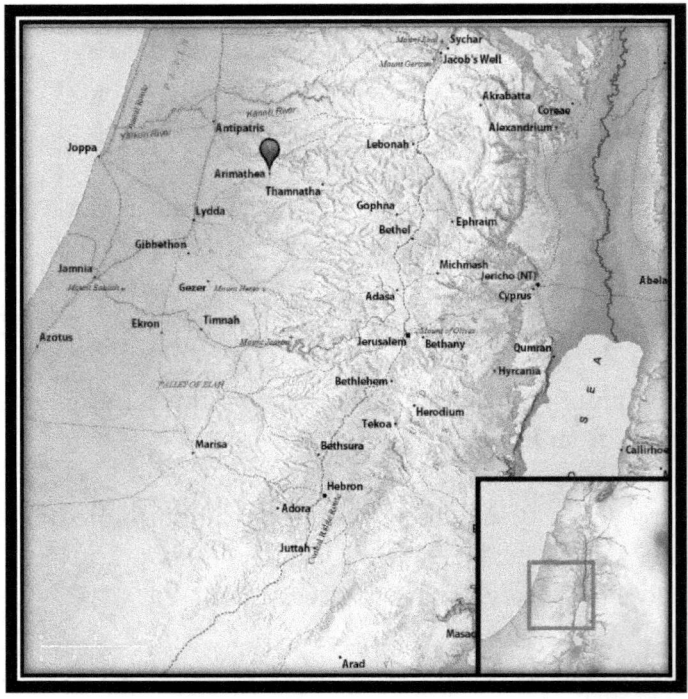

Arimathea
Isaacology.com. [2018] Arimathea
[Accessed 2018]

Albert Einstein was right; everything in God, and for God's people, is predetermined.

Now the tomb is empty.

The Empty Tomb of Jesus -

Gettyimages.co.uk. Chapel of Jacobites and Tomb of Joseph of Arimathea [Accessed 2018]

It is amazing, awesome grace, to be in the plans of God.

Lord, I love the habitation of your house and the place where your glory dwells [Psalms 26:8].

CHAPTER 12

THE LORD OUR HABITATION

Fiercely Faithful

From the stories told by Moses, to the narrations of John the Revelator, God is so faithful.

The Psalmist says,

The word of Jehovah is right; And all his work is done in faithfulness **[Psalms 33:4]**.

Our God does not change.

He is forever faithful.

Moses says to the children of Israel,

God is not a man, that he should lie; neither the son of man, that he should repent: hath he said, and shall he not do it? or hath he spoken, and shall he not make it good **[Numbers 23:19]**.

As children of God, we take the word of our father as is.

Challenges will come, but we are only strong in our God.

We are strong in Jesus.

The Bible says,

But as many as received him, to them gave he power to become the sons of God, even to them that believe on his name [John 1:12].

As Paul would then say to the Hebrews,

15 And for this cause he is the mediator of a new covenant, that a death having taken place for the redemption of the transgressions that were under the first covenant, they that have been called may receive the promise of the eternal inheritance [Hebrews 9:15].

To Paul, we can only give glory to God the Father,

²⁴ And to Jesus the mediator of the new covenant, and to the blood of sprinkling, that speaketh better things than that of Abel [Hebrews 12:24].

Jesus is the only way to the Father.

For character fit, the Lord God says to Joshua,

This book of the law shall not depart out of thy mouth; but thou shalt meditate therein day and night, that thou mayest observe to do according to all that is written *therein: for then thou shalt make thy way prosperous, and then thou shalt have good success. ⁹Have not I commanded thee? Be strong and of a good courage; be not afraid, neither be thou dismayed: for the LORD thy God is with thee whithersoever thou goest **[Joshua in 1:8-9]**.*

The book of the law is the Word of God.

The Word guarantees. Whithersoever just means any place and any space, God is with us.

To the children of Israel He says,

Withersoever,

> 1. 'Tis so sweet to trust in Jesus,
> Just to take Him at His Word;
> Just to rest upon His promise,
> And to know, "Thus saith the Lord!"
>
> o *Refrain:*
> Jesus, Jesus, how I trust Him!
> How I've proved Him o'er and o'er;
> Jesus, Jesus, precious Jesus!
> Oh, for grace to trust Him more!
>
> 2. Oh, how sweet to trust in Jesus,
> Just to trust His cleansing blood;
> And in simple faith to plunge me
> 'Neath the healing, cleansing flood!

3. Yes, 'tis sweet to trust in Jesus,
   Just from sin and self to cease;
   Just from Jesus simply taking
   Life and rest, and joy and peace.

4. I'm so glad I learned to trust Thee,
   Precious Jesus, Savior, Friend;
   And I know that Thou art with me,
   Wilt be with me to the end.

Louisa M.R. Stead 1882
Timeless Truths Free Online Library

Jesus – The Lord Protector

God is in our situations because we are not of our own.

We belong to God, God created and God saved.

The Lord our God makes it easier, to do His will. The Lord says,

And I will put my spirit within you, and cause you to walk in my statutes, and ye shall keep my judgments, and do them [Ezekiel 36: 27].

We cannot on our own, we have never on our own and we will never on our own.

The Word of the Lord says to Jeremiah,

Can the Ethiopian change his skin, or the leopard his spots? then may ye also do good, that are accustomed to do evil [Jeremiah 13:23].

God has done everything for us. He has put his Spirit in us, to whisper to us the things of God.

We can be Godly, because God gently causes us to walk in His Word.

Jesus says, a*t that day ye shall know that I am in my Father, and ye in me, and I in you [John 14:20].*

This is the conspiracy of heaven.

Paul says this Word will protect us,

[14] Seeing then that we have a great high priest, that is passed into the heavens, Jesus the Son of God, let us hold fast our profession. [15] For we have not an high priest which cannot be touched with the feeling of our infirmities; but was in all points tempted like as we are, yet without sin. [16] Let us therefore come boldly unto the throne of grace, that we may obtain mercy, and find grace to help in time of need [Hebrews 4:14-16].

What we do is claim the promises of God. We Pray.

He said so to the children of Israel taken into captivity, and He says to us too.

The Lord our God *will*. Not in our time, but in His time.

The Lord Our Habitation

The Bible says,

Delight thyself also in the LORD: and he shall give thee the desires of thine heart. For he hath looked down from the height of his sanctuary; from heaven did the LORD behold the earth [Psalm 37:4-5].

The assurance is real.

To Moses, even after Marah, the Bible says,

And Moses went up from the plains of Moab unto the mountain of Nebo, to the top of Pisgah, that is over against Jericho. And the LORD shewed him all the land of Gilead, unto Dan, ² And all Naphtali, and the land of Ephraim, and Manasseh, and all the land of Judah, unto the utmost sea, ³ And the south, and the plain of the valley of Jericho, the city of palm trees, unto Zoar. ⁴ And the LORD said unto him, This is the land which I sware unto Abraham, unto Isaac, and unto Jacob, saying, I will give it unto thy seed: I have caused thee to see it with thine eyes, but thou shalt not go over thither. ⁵ So Moses the servant of the LORD died there in the land of Moab, according to the word of the LORD. ⁶ And he buried him in a valley in the land of

Moab, over against Bethpeor: but no man knoweth of his sepulchre unto this day. ⁷ And Moses was an hundred and twenty years old when he died: his eye was not dim, nor his natural force abated ***[Deuteronomy 34:1-7].***

Moses died at the top of the mountain, with twenty/twenty vision.

Moses saw the whole of Canaan, whilst on top of the mountain,

Moses would not have walked to see the whole of Canaan if he had not walked to the top of Mt Pisgah.

That was grace.

Hannah says of God,

He will keep the feet of his saints, and the wicked shall be silent in darkness; for by strength shall no man prevail ***[1 Samuel 2:9].***

To Isaiah our God said,

I will go before thee, and make the crooked places straight: I will break in pieces the gates of brass, and cut in sunder the bars of iron ***[Isaiah 45:2-4].***

To Jeremiah, the Lord said,

And I will make thee unto this people a fenced brasen wall: and they shall fight against thee, but they shall not prevail against thee: for I am with thee to save thee and to deliver thee, saith the LORD. ^{21} And I will deliver thee out of the hand of the wicked, and I will redeem thee out of the hand of the terrible. [Jeremiah 15:20-21].

To Paul God said,

My grace is sufficient for thee: for my strength is made perfect in weakness [2 Corinthians 12:9].

David, about God he said,

The LORD bringeth the counsel of the heathen to nought: he maketh the devices of the people of none effect [Psalm 33:10].

Behold, the eye of the LORD is upon them that fear him, upon them that hope in his mercy; ^{19} To deliver their soul from death, and to keep them alive in famine. [Psalm 33:18-19].

As much as the Lord spoke to the children of Israel, He also says to us,

^{6} For I am the LORD, I change not..;^{7} Return unto me, and I will return unto you, ...^{13} Your words have been stout against me, saith the LORD. Yet ye say, What have

*we spoken so much against thee? ⁱ⁴ Ye have said, It is vain to serve God: and what profit is it that we have kept his ordinance,...¹⁶ Then they that feared the LORD spake often one to another: and the LORD hearkened, and heard it, and a book of remembrance was written before him for them that feared the LORD, and that thought upon his name **[Malachi 3:6-16].***

Our God does not change, what He did for Hannah, He will do it for you and for me.

What He said to Isaiah, He also says to you and to me.

What He did for Jeremiah, He will do it for you and for me.

It is not in vain that we worship God.

Lord, I love the habitation of your house and the place where your glory dwells [Psalms 26:8].

CHAPTER 13

INEXHAUSTIBLE GRACE

Fearing and worshipping God is not transactional.

God is God. It is not a business relationship; it is the essence of life.

The Bible says,

Be still, and know that I am God: I will be exalted among the heathen; I will be exalted in the earth ***[Psalm 46:10]***.

And Isaiah boldly says,

But they that wait upon the LORD shall renew their strength; they shall mount up with wings as eagles; they shall run, and not be weary; and they shall walk, and not faint ***[Isaiah 40:31]***.

Wait, wait upon the Lord.

Be strong, firm, standing unmovable, on the strength of the Word of God.

His grace is sufficient.
Above All

Paul says to the Ephesians – stand.

This is a very short word that does not need interpretation or explanation.

We are not built for condemnation, for one who builds us in an excellent builder; He is also the chief cornerstone.

Our foundation is sure, and as Paul says in Hebrews,

But we are not of them who draw back unto perdition; but of them that believe to the saving of the soul ***[Hebrews 10:39].***

How we stand will determine how high we can go.

A building will stand on its foundation.

Our foundation is Christ, the Way to the Father.

That is why Paul says,

^{14} Stand therefore, having your loins girt about with truth, and having on the breastplate of righteousness; ^{15} And your feet shod with the preparation of the gospel of peace; ^{16} Above all, taking the shield of faith, wherewith ye shall be able to quench all the fiery darts of the wicked. ^{17} And take the helmet of salvation, and

the sword of the Spirit, which is the word of God: ¹⁸ Praying always with all prayer and supplication in the Spirit, and watching thereunto with all perseverance and supplication for all saints; ***[Ephesians 6:10-18].***

These weapons of our warfare are not carnal, but mighty through God, for the pulling down of strongholds.

Paul says,

*For the weapons of our warfare are not carnal, but mighty through God to the pulling down of strong holds; ⁵ Casting down imaginations, and every high thing that exalteth itself against the knowledge of God, and bringing into captivity every thought to the obedience of Christ **[2 Corinthians 10:4-5].***

*Being confident of this very thing, that he [God] which hath begun a good work in you [us] will perform it until the day of Jesus Christ **[Philippians 1:6].***

Standing does not mean what comes will not come; it means we will not be intimidated, because we have made the Lord, the Creator of the Universe, the Giver of life, our habitation.

It means we keep tagged to the rope that connects us to our power source.

It means we put on the whole armour of God.

It means praying without season.

There is and there will be grace in everything we come across, as children of God.

We keep building, brick on brick, steel on steel, hewing our graves on the rock of all ages – Jesus the Christ.

Jesus is the story of grace.

Lord, I love the habitation of your house and the place where your glory dwells [Psalms 26:8].

CHAPTER 14

CONCLUSION

Fitly Framed Together

Everyone builds, for Pharaoh, for self, people build.

Building is not wrong, because God said for us to occupy till He comes.

Building for God is just different. It is building character, it is building life, it is building hope, and it is building for eternity.

Our Lord Jesus says, *am the vine, ye* are *the branches: He that abideth in me, and I in him, the same bringeth forth much fruit: for without me ye can do nothing* ***[John 15:5]***.

When Jesus builds, there are no tilted buildings or tilted characters.

If the tilt should come, God says put forward your case, let us reason together. There is no greater grace.

Moses tilted at the waters of Marah, but God gave grace. Marah became the place of laughter, of happiness.

Paul was tilted, before grace found him. David too, till God created in him a new heart.

The Lord God then says,

*I am Alpha and Omega, the beginning and the ending, saith the Lord, which is, and which was, and which is to come, the Almighty **[Revelation 8:1]**.*

*In whom [Christ] ALL the building fitly framed together groweth unto an holy temple in the Lord: [22] In whom ye also are builded together for an habitation of God through the Spirit. **[Ephesians 2:21-22]**.*

The story of building, from Noah, to Moses, to Joseph of Arimathea is fitly framed together.

This is the ultimate story. There is no better story to tell.

Isaiah asks – who shall believe this story, because it truly is an awesome story.

Throughout the generations of human existence, we shall

Sing unto the LORD, all the earth; [24] Declare his glory among the heathen; his marvellous works among all nations. [25] For great is the LORD, and greatly to be praised.... the LORD made the heavens. [27] Glory and honour are in his presence; strength and gladness are *in his place……Give unto the LORD the glory due unto his name: ……worship the LORD in the beauty of holiness **[1 Chronicles 16:23-29]**.*

*And all things are of God, who hath reconciled us to himself by Jesus Christ **[2 Corinthians 5:18]**.*

We all are builders, in one way or the other.

I have preferred to tell this story, the story I know, the story of God's grace.

> All things bright and beautiful,
> All creatures great and small,
> All things wise and wonderful:
> The Lord God made them all.
>
> Each little flow'r that opens,
> Each little bird that sings,
> He made their glowing colours,
> He made their tiny wings.
>
> The purple-headed mountains,
> The river running by,
> The sunset and the morning
> That brightens up the sky.
>
> The cold wind in the winter,
> The pleasant summer sun,
> The ripe fruits in the garden,

He made them every one.

The tall trees in the greenwood,
The meadows where we play,
The rushes by the water,
To gather every day.

He gave us eyes to see them,
And lips that we might tell
How great is God Almighty,
Who has made all things well.

Cecil F. Alexander 1848
Timeless Truths Free Online Library

This narration captures inspiring chapters and verses of the Bible from Moses to John.

It is my story too, in honour and praise of my God, magnificent in all His works and the source of inexhaustible grace!

As Hannah put it,

For by strength shall no man prevail.

Lord, I love the habitation of your house and the place where your glory dwells [Psalms 26:8].

REFERENCES

Typical Building Site -
Business Media. [2018]. *Panelization Takes Command.* [online]. Available at: www.canadianarchitect.com/features/panelization-takes-command/attachment/1002223777-1002223829/[Accessed 2018].

Definition of Power-
Google.com. [2018]. *What is power.* [online]. Available at: www.google.co.zw/search?q=what+is+power&oq=what+is+power&aqs=chrome..69i57j0l5.4027j1j4&sourceid=chrome&ie=UTF-8 [Accessed 2018].

John of Patmos –
Greeka.com.*Patmos History.* [online]. Available at: www.greeka.com/dodecanese/patmos/patmos-history.htm [Accessed 2018].

Island of Patmos Location –
The Skibbereen Eagle. [December 28, 2014]. *Revelation, Apocalypse and The Island of Patmos.* [online]. Available at: http://www.skibbereeneagle.ie/uncategorized/revelation-apocalypse-island-patmos/ [Accessed 2018].

Definition of Mind –
Wikipedia.org. [January, 2019]. *Mind.* [online]. Available at: https://en.wikipedia.org/wiki/Mind [Accessed 2018].

Interesting Facts About The Pyramids of Giza –
Facts Legend. [December1, 2015]. *Great Pyramid of Giza – 60 Interesting Facts To Blow Your Mind.* [online]. Available at: https://factslegend.org/great-pyramid-of-giza-60-interesting-facts-to-blow-your-mind/ [Accessed 2018].

Witnesses –
Justice.gov.nt.ca. *Going to court as a witness or victim in a criminal matter.* [online]. Available at:
https://www.justice.gov.nt.ca/en/going-to-court-as-a-witness-or-victim/ [Accessed 2018].

The Foundations of the Leaning Tower of Pisa-
Expedia. [2018]. *Leaning Tower.* [online]. Available at: https://www.expedia.com/Leaning-Tower-Pisa.d6270669.Vacation-Attraction [Accessed October 12, 2018].

Leaning Tower of Pisa –
Wikipedia.org. [January 29, 2018]. *Leaning Tower of Pisa.* [online]. Available at:
https://en.wikipedia.org/wiki/Leaning_Tower_of_Pisa [Accessed October 12, 2018].

Characteristics of the Desert-
Wikipedia.org. [July 26, 2018]. *Desert.* [online]. Available at: https://en.wikipedia.org/wiki/Desert [Accessed 2018].

Parker Solar Probe –
NASA. [July 20, 2018]. *NASA Prepares to Launch Parker Solar Probe, a Mission to Touch the Sun.* [online]. Available at: https://www.nasa.gov/feature/goddard/2018/nasa-prepares-to-launch-parker-solar-probe-a-mission-to-touch-the-sun [Accessed November 9, 2018].

Tower of Babel –
Wikipedia.org. [September 4, 2018]. *Tower of Babel.* [online]. Available at: https://en.wikipedia.org/wiki/Tower_of_Babel [Accessed November 9, 2018].

Pyramids of Egypt –
Wikipedia.org. [December 30, 2018]. *Egyptian Pyramids.* [online]. Available at: https://en.wikipedia.org/wiki/Egyptian_pyramids [Accessed October 12, 2018].

The Great Pyramid of Giza –
Benjamin Lampkin. [February 9.2016]. *12 Wondorous Facts about the great Pyramid of Giza.* [online]. Available at: http://mentalfloss.com/article/75076/12-wondrous-facts-about-great-pyramid-giza [Accessed October 12, 2018].

Tallest Buildings –
K. Haider. [May 11, 2015]. *5 Tallest Buildings in the World.* [online]. Available at: https://www.ubergizmo.com/articles/tallest-buildings/ [Accessed October 12, 2018].

Mandarin Duck –
Puzzle Warehouse. [2017]. *Exotics – Mandarin Duck.* [online]. Available at: https://www.puzzlewarehouse.com/Exotics-Mandarin-Duck-50935aan-2.html [Accessed December 12, 2018].

Rearguard –
Wikipedia.org. [October 23, 2018]. *Rearguard.* [online]. Available at: https://en.wikipedia.org/wiki/Rearguard [Accessed November 21, 2018].

Dunkirk –
Wikipedia.org. [October 3, 2018]. *Battle of Dunkirk.* [online]. Available at: https://en.wikipedia.org/wiki/Battle_of_Dunkirk [Accessed November 21, 2018].

Solomon's Temple –
Freegracekids.com. *Lesson 19-Solomon-The Temple and Sanctification.* [online]. Available at:
https://freegracekids.com/2018/01/29/lesson-19-solomon-the-temple-and-sanctification/ [Accessed November 23, 2018].

Poverty in Pictures-
E. Vuong. [July 11, 2014]. *Measuring Global Poverty.* [online]. Available at: http://economicstudents.com/2014/07/measuring-global-poverty/ [Accessed November 29, 2018].

Poverty and Hunger –
A.Porter [April 5, 2017]. *Extreme poverty set to rise across Southern Africa.* [online]. Available at: https://issafrica.org/iss-today/extreme-poverty-set-to-rise-across-southern-africa [Accessed November 29, 2018].

Masai Ostrich –
Wikipedia.org. [September 1, 2009]. *Male Ostrich in Ngorongoro.* [online]. Available at:
https://en.wikipedia.org/wiki/Masai_ostrich#/media/File:Ostrich_Ngorongoro_05.jpg [Accessed December 2018].

Horse Speed –
Wikipedia.org. [November 15, 2018]. *Fastest Animals.* [online]. Available at: https://en.wikipedia.org/wiki/Fastest_animals [Accessed December 4, 2018].

Horse Power –
Lemen.com. [2006]. *Questions and Answers.* [online]. Available at: http://www.lemen.com/qa221.html [Accessed December 4, 2018].

Appaloosa Horse –
Wkipedia.org. [October 15, 2018]. *Appaloosa.* [online]. Available at: https://en.wikipedia.org/wiki/Appaloosa [Accessed December 4, 2018].

Noah's Ark –
Pininterest.com. *The Ark on Mount Ararat.* [online]. Available at: https://www.pinterest.com/pin/339318153171492270/?lp=true [Accessed January 29, 2019].

Arimathea –
Isaacology.com. [2018]. *Arimathea.* [online]. Available at: http://www.isaacology.com/En/ViewMaps?M=1519041205 [Accessed 2018].

Mt Ararat –
Worldwideflood.com. [December 2005]. *Why Mt Ararat.* [online]. Available at: http://worldwideflood.com/flood/ararat/ararat.htm [Accessed 2018].

The Empty Tomb of Jesus -
Gettyimages.co.uk. *Chapel of Jacobites and Tomb of Joseph of Arimathea.* [online]. Available at: [Accessed 2018].

Mind Power –
Google.com. *Mind Power.* [online]. Available at: https://www.google.co.zw/search?q=the+power+of+the+mind&oq=the+power+of+the+mind&aqs=chrome..69i57j0l5.5538j0j7&sourceid=chrome&ie=UTF-8 [Accessed November 7, 2018].

Typical Desert –
Google.com. *Typical Desert.* [online]. Available at: https://www.google.com/search?biw=1366&bih=657&tbm=isch&sa=1&ei=ZY8YXIOuL7D5sAfjyo7QBg&q=typical+desert+

&oq=typical+desert+&gs_l=img.3..35i39j0j0i30j0i24l5.7996.9495..10372...0.0..0.406.2171.2-7j0j1......1....1..gws-wiz-img.HVztnyimWSA#imgrc=-tX_nZ5oIA26LM: [Accessed October 12, 2018].

Burj Khalifa
Destination Dubai. [2016]. *Modern Dubai +Burj Khalifa Guide Tour.* [online]. Available at: http://destination-dubai.fr/en/guided-tours/107-modern-dubai-burj-khalifa-guided-tour.html [Accessed October 2018].

OTHER BOOKS BY THE AUTHOR:

- CHAPTERS OF CHRISTIAN LIFE
- ALONE WITH GOD IN 22 STEPS
  - Proverbs 31-
- THE LOST DRACHMA
  - Love -
- HE IS COMING BACK
- PHARAOH'S HORSES AND HIS CHARIOTS
- A TESTIMONY OF OUR FAITH